WHAT PEOPLE ARE SAYING ABOUT

HOLE

This is an engaging b̶c̶ ⎯son, and
crossing genres of criticism, confession, analysis and polemic. It
provokes the reader to think about urbanism as a dynamic
intellectual field of ideas and experiences. Specialists and general
readers will find this book stimulating as the author leaps around
from idea to idea, always provocative and always full of insights.
He relates issues in architecture, the city and urban life to a range
of historical philosophical and cultural issues – from justice and
ethics to creativity and community, public space and violence.
There are few writers who take such a synthetic and wide-
ranging approach in the English speaking world. Moreover, it
intellectually reconnects Europe's East and West, introducing a
sense of flair into an overly laboured field of academic research.
Dr Jonathan Vickery, Associate Professor, Director MA Global
Media and Communication, Centre for Cultural Policy Studies
University of Warwick

A refreshing book. In a context where only 'world cities' matter to
most urbanists, Krzysztof Nawratek is a thinker equally at home
writing about Katowice and Shanghai, London and Plymouth. In
this unromantic, lapidary but ultimately optimistic work he offers
a precise diagnosis of contemporary urban ills and offers some
potential ways out of some worn-out ways of thinking the city.
Never mind worrying about the Polis or the decline of public
space – this book calls instead for a revolutionary new urbanism.
Owen Hatherley, author of *Militant Modernism, A Guide to New
Ruins of Great Britain* and *A New Kind of Bleak: Journeys Through
Urban Britain.*

Holes in the Whole

Introduction to the Urban Revolutions

Holes in
the Whole

Introduction to the Urban Revolutions

Krzysztof Nawratek

Winchester, UK
Washington, USA

First published by Zero Books, 2012
Zero Books is an imprint of John Hunt Publishing Ltd., Laurel House, Station Approach,
Alresford, Hants, SO24 9JH, UK
office1@jhpbooks.net
www.johnhuntpublishing.com
www.zero-books.net

For distributor details and how to order please visit the 'Ordering' section on our website.

Text copyright: Krzysztof Nawratek 2012

ISBN: 978 1 78099 375 1

A CIP catalogue record for this book is available from the British Library.

Translated from Polish into English by Kasia Nawratek

Design: Stuart Davies

Printed and bound by CPI Group (UK) Ltd, Croydon, CR0 4YY

We operate a distinctive and ethical publishing philosophy in all
areas of our business, from our global network of authors to
production and worldwide distribution.

CONTENTS

Why urban revolutions?

Recent years have brought a growing interest – even a fascination – with the city. A certain change in how cities are talked and written about can also be observed. This change is about growing optimism and the belief that the best time for cities is yet to come. A good example of this is a book by Edward Glaeser released in 2011, in the midst of the ongoing crisis, entitled 'Triumph of the city'. The title speaks for itself. Another characteristic example is a book by Nan Ellin, who quotes Saskia Sassen, Richard Florida and Alvin Toffler (a known anti-urbanist[1]) in her book 'Integral Urbanism' to impress upon the reader the belief that the modern city is in good condition.

Similarly, in another book published at the top of the speculative real estate bubble, 'Social Economy of the Metropolis. Cognitive-Cultural Capitalism and the Global Resurgence of Cities', Allen J. Scottt puts forward the dual argument (which is representative of this optimistic view on the future of cities and therefore worth discussing) that cities are the effect of capitalism and its natural environment. Cognitive, knowledge-based capitalism is then to bring about the golden era of the city. There are hundreds of books presenting the same argument in different variants. Can so many authors be wrong?[2]

In my opinion yes[3], and for anyone who is familiar with my previous book it shouldn't be a surprise. Cities are not alright and this diagnosis is a starting point for this book. Indeed the problem of modern western cities is that they exist only by the power of inertia or are rapidly shrinking (the phenomenon of 'shrinking cities' in Germany or the United States). There are cities, like Berlin, whose existence is solely based on political will. There is no industry in Berlin but there are a lot of people who could be included in the 'creative class'. According to those who still believe Richard Florida, this is a city that should flourish. It is true that Berlin is a good place to live, especially for young people seeking cultural entertainment. Unfortunately it is the German state that is paying for this good life – Berlin is heavily indebted and unable to live without the financial state drip. There are also cities that are nothing more but big playgrounds of consumption and entertainment, such as Dubai and Wolfsburg.

Although Alvin Toffler is no longer fashionable today[4], his predictions of escape from major urban centres seem to be accurate. The main reason for this is the way that knowledge is produced and distributed in the knowledge based economy of today. Contrary to the previously mentioned thesis of Alan Scott, it appears that cognitive capitalism doesn't work for the city: today, 'creative cities' are indebted cities[5]. It seems then that the fascination with fluidity and creativity, with art and culture as driving forces of modern urban development is a kind of delusion, having little to do with what modern cities are and what their future may be.

It is worthwhile to stop for a moment and to try to explain the reasons for the widespread belief that today cities are at their peak. Indeed, most of the world's income is generated in cities[6]; it is, however, difficult to put this observation into the context of the financial and fiscal crisis that first hit cities at the end of the 1970s and which has been deepening since 2008. As I wrote in 'City as a political idea', it is not cities but urban areas that can be successful. This distinction is crucial – cities are not entities in an economical and political sense. They no longer decide their own fate and have instead become a resource of space, buildings, infrastructure and people (as consumers and employees). These resources are utilised by phenomena transcendent to cities – mainly global corporations.

European and North American cities are mostly defined as post-industrial. After the fall of industry, or its export to Asia, what remains in these cities is still unfilled holes in space (brownfield sites) and social tissue (the redundant working class). Today, most of these cities in the West are shrinking, with very few exceptions such as London or Paris, while Asian, South American and African cities are growing. It is important to realise that these growing cities are not post-industrial, but – especially in China – their success comes from combining strengths of the industrial city with the city as the centre of knowledge production and consumption. However, even growing cities – although in different ways to cities in the West – are mostly unable to exercise power over themselves. Spaces controlled by global corporations, the state (military sites, roads, railways) and natural reserves protected by international agreements (such as European Union areas protected by the programme Natura 2000) are beyond the control of the city authorities. I would then risk the thesis that contrary to optimists who see a bright future for our cities', one can have doubts whether there is any future for cities at all. This doubt stems from the fact that in contrast to fortified forts, market towns and even cities from the industrial era, cities today do not seem necessary at all.

The city is unnecessary and its artificiality is perfectly visible in Dubai and Las Vegas. Dubai is almost perfectly apolitical – only 10% of its population have local citizenship[7] while Las Vegas[8] is a city that lives almost entirely from consumption. Both Dubai and Las Vegas are cities serving as playgrounds for people from other, 'real' cities – if they exist.

Dubai is an artificially calculated city-like product. It is a trap for a modern consumer, selling emotions and orgiastic excitement. It is, however, exceptional in its reaction to the 2009 crisis. When it was expected that Dubai awaited a fate similar to other global cities, 10 billion dollars from Abu Dhabi restored its financial stability. Today it is again, albeit on a smaller scale, a place attracting investors[9]. However, it seems that it wasn't that Dubai the city survived the crisis; rather it was the financial structures of the Arab world that saved it.

A question arises: What in fact is the raison d'être of the city? Is there anything unique produced in the city? It isn't food – it may be vital for us to survive, but (with few exceptions) it is produced outside the city. Neither is it industrial products, as the industrial city is the product of a bygone era. Today production (in the West) takes place outside cities, in industrial clusters or high-technology zones, drawing inspiration from Silicon Valley, which, after all, is not a city.

The most archaic feature of the city as a place where the culture, language and codes of a society – thus power – is produced. Today culture is also produced on the Internet, in isolation from any city or physical locality.

For years, the city was defined as 'a densely populated area of permanent residence, in which food is not produced'. Today, from Havana to Detroit even this dogma is being questioned. What then does determine the city – even as a resource, not a subject – as a phenomenon? What makes it unique?

The answers we are looking for lie in the number of inhabitants of the city and the density of interactions. It is helpful to refer to Adam Smiths classic theses concerning the division of labour in order to understand that the phenomenon of the city comes in fact from millions of small subsystems, based on their own and often distinctly different logic and interwoven with each other into a bigger system. In the city these subsystems are easily accessible not only because physical distances are small, but also because the language-interface, which subsystems use to communicate with each other, is more or less codified in a given city. The language-interface is one of the key concepts that I will be using in this book and a more detailed explanation will appear in following chapters. At the moment, an intuitive understanding of the language can be used; we will define it as a medium allowing for exchange of information and engaging in effective relationships.

Very often, especially when we talk about financial opera-
tions, it is definitely closer from Wall Street in New York to
London City than from the City to Peckham, one of the poorest
areas of London. Both the accessibility and the language which
financial centres use to communicate with each other can make
the bond between two geographically distant places stronger
than that between two districts of the same city. The city can
therefore be seen as a locality, but one defined by proximity in
terms of accessibility and interface, not necessarily associated
with spatial location.

In the 1990s a dispute erupted among geographers about 'the
end of geography[10], which well illustrated the fascination with
technology, the dominance of finance over industrial production
and the idea of non-spatial availability. However, although this
dispute cannot be resolved using the 19th century categories, it is
worth commenting on it from the meta-level using the
geographic concepts of availability and the interface for communication between fragments.

This dispute put at its centre concepts which at first glance
seem archaic but are in fact again at the centre of the current
political debate. For example, the Big Society idea promoted by
the UK's Conservative coalition government in 2010-2011 deals
with questions of locality and local community. To interpret
locality as the Conservatives do is to refer to Heidegger's (post)
phenomenological legacy with its obsession of dwelling. In its
distorted form this understanding of dwelling could be turned
against nomads such as Jews, Roma, Travellers and immigrants
in general. Obviously, recalling Heidegger it can also lead to
risky simplifications such as 'locality=Nazism'. It is tempting to
use it in an argument and however justified, it is more interesting to take a closer look at the idea of locality in this concept
instead.

There are many studies devoted to the segregation of urban
space showing strong attachment between residents to districts

they live in. It is very important to realise that this locality was to some (often significant!) degree forced. People used to live and work next to each other because they belonged to a particular social class, ethnic or religious group. It was in fact an exact transfer of the rural social structure into the urban environment. This understanding of locality in the city has changed as we do not trust our neighbours now as much as in the past and – both result and factor of this – because life in the city is not confined to one district only. People live and work in different parts of the city; they send their children to schools in other districts and all of it is possible because of efficient transport links within the city. Some places get new roads and some don't, some places get free Internet access and some don't – it is the act of communication that is important, not its nature. Locality then has not disappeared and even if now people have more in common with their Facebook friends than with their next door neighbours, it is still the connection between them that matters. However, it cannot be seen in the banal dichotomy of the geographical versus the virtual.

Local community is in some ways a step back: it can very easily describe people not in relation to others but in opposition to them. The local community was (and still is, especially in deprived areas) primarily founded on a shared fear of 'the outside'. Such communities have strong social capital but their inhabitants are poorly integrated with extra-local social networks. It is also the biggest difference between disadvantaged neighbourhoods and more affluent areas.

Both leftist utopians and rightist communitarians yearn for a district with strong local community. This idea, known as 'sustainable community', was promoted in the UK by the Labour government and today in the form of the Big Society it has become the pillar of Conservative social policy. Unfortunately, the local community disappeared a long time ago. It disappeared, not because the demon of civilisation devoured it, but because city people themselves broke free from its bounds – at least in some places and to some extent. This does not mean, however, that all ties between people living next to each other have disappeared or that something bad has happened.

The association 'Us Poznanians'[11], highly successful in local elections with almost 10% of votes and visibly present in local media, was founded as one of many associations attracting people who wanted to influence the future of their city. The association is structured as a network of local groups and because of this form it was able to overcome limitations of district-centred thinking. It was its networking nature that enabled thinking and acting not only on the level of a district but also expanded its focus to other districts and even the whole city. This dual nature of 'Us Poznanians' gives us a clue to what is or what may be the modern city. On the one hand there is a local, egoistic interest in defending a certain territory and we can extend this thinking in the direction of intimacy. Such intimacy with a place is built over time and with a slowly gathered knowledge of people, objects, and space. This intimate relationship may contain an element of possessiveness – 'This is MY place' – but I would rather focus on this intimate tenderness people build *between* themselves and a place, not the egoistic act of possession.

This intimate tenderness is worth defending. Because it concerns the relationship between us and other people or a place (an object), by its very nature it forces us to step out of ourselves and reach out. Any ethics starts where something beyond us becomes more important than ourselves. Ethics then requires transcendence and in the urban context, extension – but not rejection – of locality.

Locality as intimacy is therefore not limited to physical space – thanks to the development of the communication technology it is often easier to find friends and 'neighbours' on the other side of the globe than next door. Even if we get to know our closest neighbours it very often happens through our Internet networks[12]. Technology can reveal and expose those parts of ourselves that remain hidden during accidental encounters in a local park or a café. It is the Internet however where our personality is revealed but not our physicality. Jacek Dukaj wrote that online we are 'in spirit', in the flesh we are 'in filth'[13]. Is then locality based on physical contact a thing of the past? Richard Sennett writes in 'Flesh and Stone'[14] about relationships built on senses other than sight, on smell and touch. Today, these relationships do seem to be disappearing and as smell and touch are treated as violations of our privacy, we do not really miss these relationships with others. As I wrote[15] about the general principle of the local community built on need, in a sensual dimension, it is the necessity and violence that are being rejected but not sensuality as such.

It is time to discuss causes of the success of the city, however controversial this success might be. The only reason for the flourishing of modern cities is that they are nodes in global flows. It is these flows – of capital, people and ideas – that constitute the city. The city exists in its instability and any attempt to freeze the flow will bring forth its end.

Despite this, modern cities try to somehow hold on to these tides and contain them. They try doing this in different ways and focus on different aspects – from the capital, through industry, trade to people (Floridian creative capital). However, cities are aware – or at least they should be – that this strategy is doomed in the long run. Yes, for a moment they manage to attract a corporation that will build a factory but it will only be moved elsewhere after a couple of years, tempted by a better offer. Richard Florida's idea to 'trap' people who for reasons like sentiment, family, friends and their children's school, are less inclined to nomadic lifestyle cannot succeed exactly because of what creative class is. The defining characteristic of the creative class, which according to Florida is crucial for cities' success, is its mobility. By definition, the creative class is nomadic, and as much as it stimulates cities it needs stimulation itself.

Despite this, Florida's idea (in the context of the ideas of others, to name but a few in Jane Jacobs, Sharon Zukin and Edward Glaeser[16]) can be interpreted as an attempt – even if only partial – to restore the city as an entity, as a subject. Despite all objections to Florida's concept, his idea of the creative class is not some kind of esoteric flow, but living people. And living people with their needs and weaknesses have to be the foundation of thinking about the city. So perhaps 'the spirit' is tied with 'the filth'.

The city, however, exists, even though it is unnecessary, even though it is built on the lie (I am using here the word *lie* in reference to the lie as used by Jacek Dukaj[17]). In Dukaj's terms, to lie in this meaning is to *lie yourself* beyond your 'natural' state, created by external conditions and innate characteristics. Arguments for the constitutive and life-giving lie, as tenderness protecting form brutality of truth, as creativity and freedom, can be found in many places – from 'The Watchmen' to the works of Harold Bloom and Agata Bielik-Robson. Just as Bloom describes the offensive-defensive strategies of a subject, which by the act of fantasising about its own existence and power creates them[18], so does the city. It lies itself into necessity of being. The city was always a surplus and it has always created the need for its own existence.

If I expose the weakness and the lack of necessity of the city it is not because of any anti-urban bias I might hold. It is exactly the opposite – yet again I call for rebuilding the city as a subject. I am calling for an even better lie. Obviously, the city still possesses remnants of attributes that justified its existence in the past. There is still industry, trade, institutions of power and knowledge in cities. However, they are just remnants of the faded glory. They exist and will continue to exist; after all, the city is a palimpsest. Perhaps the most interesting contemporary example of such a city can be found in China where layers from almost all phases of city development are still present, from the city growing fat on its feudal, rural surroundings to 'the creative city' of today. It is interesting that as early as the 1980s F. G. Castles (quoted by Jadwiga Staniszkis in 'The Ontology of Socialism') described European socialist countries as syncretic structures. However, it appears that what in Europe was an anomaly heralding the fall of socialist cities there is actually the essence of the Chinese model.

However, it seems that syncretism is not enough and as it turned out to be unstable in Europe, then it cannot be everlasting in Asia too. It seems that in general cities face the challenge of adding one more layer, of undergoing the next mutation, inventing themselves anew.

The weakness of the modern city is primarily the result of cities being more of a condensation of global flows (flows of information, capital, people, ideas, etc.) than autonomous entities. Management of the city takes place on many levels – political, economic, cultural, and social. Only a small part of these levels is subject to democratic control or even slightly under the control of municipal authorities. The bigger the city, the more control gets blurred. Paul Hirts[19] writes about mega-cities (Sao Paolo) as anti-cities, where effective power is lost. As I wrote earlier, cities are not able to effectively manage themselves and therefore the urban political community has no raison d'être. It is of course possible to take matters into your own hands and when the power weakens take control over fragments of the city. Examples include the creation of guerrilla parks[20] or making a temporary art installation permanent, but all these activities prove to be ineffective sooner or later.

First of all, these are desperate measures, which anarchise the city even further. They do not reinforce subjectivity; they only deconstruct it in a more sympathetic manner than developers or global corporations. It may seem that the only way to reinstate the city as a subject is to gain a share in real power. At a basic level, such a statement is a simple call for participation in elections and political life as this is the only sphere in which citizens (at least who hold voting rights) are institutionally granted a part of the political system of the city and consequently hold potential influence on its social and economical system. Any artistic or social activity can be effective only if it becomes a part of a political struggle. However, this appeal is too banal to be effective. It is because power gained through elections still has the ability to influence the city's structures. The real problem begins with the next step. Say the elections were won – what next?

True urban change, the necessity of which has been demonstrated by my previous comments, does not begin with gaining power. It starts with understanding the mechanisms, which will allow restoration of the city's subjectivity and will regain the power to shape the city's own destiny and future.

Freedom of creation

For change – including revolution – to be possible, freedom is of fundamental importance. So too is property: a stable relationship between man and matter (objects, places) is an essential anchor in a world swept by tides of capital, people and information. Perhaps this is why it's worth considering these two concepts – liberty and property – in the perverse understanding that has been introduced into our language by (neo)liberals.

The way these concepts function in our language today is extremely ideological – this is not necessarily a bad thing in itself. The problem lies in the fact that, widespread in the language, this ideology has become transparent. We don't see it anymore and neoliberal language is regarded as a natural way of speaking and thinking. Yet even if we don't want to reject it, perhaps it is worth considering an alternative. Pluralism – a wildly popular concept in Eastern and Central Europe in the late 1980s-90s – presents a chance to overcome this language of totality.

This was the function that the idea of pluralism served during the fall of communism, and it should be repeated today. Despite the appearance it projects, neoliberalism is characterized by profound totalitarianism, claiming the right to explain the whole world through the idea of the free market. It makes the free market the ultimate criterion of truth. For the supporters of (neo)liberalism the cliché of 'a free man making free and rational choices' is applied to everything, every aspect of human life. It is this absolute freedom and not the free market as such that lies at the foundation of their thinking. It is an abstracted, idolised and individual freedom.

This form of (neo)liberal freedom is a real threat to the living, sentient man. Not only does it exist outside the society, but also outside the body and outside human beings. For the followers of absolute freedom only an individual making a free choice can be fully human – any entanglement, an addiction or dependent conditions are rejected as irrelevant. Neoliberal freedom is rational, measured and cold. It doesn't allow space for emotions, weaknesses, heart's desires or whims. Neoliberal freedom is totalitarian – there is no escape from it, there is no excuse for those who do not indulge in it fully. Such a totalistic understanding of freedom is evident in the writings of Ayn Rand, who glorified the entrepreneur as an *Übermensch*. And yes – make no mistake – it is the Nietzschean *Übermensch*, freed from the limitations of the weak, who is a follower of this thinking.

A criticism of such a perverted freedom can begin by saying that freedom exists only to a certain extent. Nobody is completely free – either because of lack of knowledge, or because of the constraints of our body (torture will break anyone and most give in to lust), or finally because of our mind's constraints (the world we see and feel as real but each of us sees it and feels it slightly differently). Without falling into postmodern relativism, the absolutisation of freedom is a fraud, which appeals to weak minds deluding themselves that they finally have a reliable tool to deal with the world.

However, our criticism cannot lead us in the direction of rejecting freedom as a superstition and delusion. We can choose a starting point for our defence of freedom at the assertion made by libertarian absolutists that liberty is above all, the freedom of choice. We are free to buy Coke or Pepsi, we can listen to pop or jazz. Freedom of choice is by definition limited only to what is available. Freedom of choice is the freedom of the supermarket.

How can we understand the free market in a context of such freedom? The free market has a cognitive significance: it is an area in which we get to know the 'truth' about the world and ourselves. The washing powder is worth as much as someone wants to pay for it, our work is worth as much the employer is willing to pay us and finally, our worth is measured by how much we can earn. This logic obviously degrades us, but we lack the language to object to it, we know no logic other than that of the free market. Absolute freedom and the free market are becoming – or have become – a totalising rationality. Is there a way to resist?

Let us ask ourselves the question: what do we need to do to enforce this rationality on ourselves? What do we need to do with ourselves, with our mind and body, to believe in total, absolute freedom and free choice? The answer is that we need to get rid of parts of ourselves. The concept of sin as in Christian theology can be helpful in this process because it defines us as 'sinful' and 'unclean' – in search of purity we lose ourselves. This is a decisive moment – if we can get rid of our own individual desires, preferences and beliefs than we can become part of a neoliberal homogeneous society. It can even make us happy, this freedom of reduced human beings. And what about the fact that this is no freedom, just a mirage imposed by the society? After the self-executed lobotomy, doubt is impossible. On the other hand, succumbing to our individual desires and preferences takes us to exactly the same place as the lobotomy: our tastes and desires are not really 'ours'. They are the result of the work of thousands of specialists of advertising and popular imagination, but still worse is that they embody the rejection of what is social and communal. The fundamental problem seems to be a distinction between need and desire.

It is interesting that a similar conclusion can be reached by following the Christian path. The American theologian Harvey Cox[21] writes about exorcising the demons of modern man to make him truly free, also from greed. But freedom, according to Cox, is not an absolute freedom but a continuation of the divine work of creation. Cox recalls the Bible passage in which man names animals and therefore cooperates with God in the act of creation.

Cox's proposal seems more convincing than a simple 'extreme liberation': what in essence could be a more radical proposal of freedom than the freedom of rational choice? Would it be the freedom of succumbing to conditions, tastes and emotions, an unlimited freedom? The error would be again similar – instead of a liberal who accepts the mirage of the rational mind making free choices, we would end up with a libertine, who believes that by following his body's desires he becomes free. Both the freedom of the liberal and the freedom of the libertarian are bound to this world; they remain enclosed within what is known. Freedom according to Cox is the freedom to create, the freedom that goes beyond the world as we know it. But such freedom is associated with danger, it is fragile and sensitive, it also brings about responsibility. It is the freedom of revolution in a phase of building, not negation, which takes responsibility for newly conquered territories. The freedom of choice is then a closed freedom, and a truly transgressive freedom is the one of creation.

There is another problem with absolute freedom: it does not concern a person – it is even beyond a person. (In this way it is like the freedom of a liberal, located in the universal rationality). Alternatively, it is only a part of a person (as in the freedom of a libertine, which isolates the freedom of the individual from other people). The personalistic perspective puts a human being in context. It doesn't reduce it, but neither does it deify its distinctiveness. On the contrary, it balances being separate and being with others. The personalistic perspective is inclusive and dialectical – the man is both individual and part of a larger whole.

In liberal ideology the relationship between freedom and property represented by Locke and Hobbs (and neoliberalism is a worthy heir to this tradition) constitutes a citizen through property. In Britain this fact is obvious – until the reform of electoral law in 1867 the right to vote (and thus the right to participate in the political community) was dependent on owning your own home. Today, property ownership continues to determine an individual's position in society. Mariusz Turowski goes even further saying simply: '...property is free, not the owner'. A little experiment can help us understand how deeply this thinking is rooted in political discourse. Let us compare arguments for and against the rights of tenants. On the one hand we have 'life'; on the other, 'capital'. It is the act of owning that constitutes the owner – all his other attributes are irrelevant. Arguments that try to give tenants preference over owners, and therefore give preference to life over capital, are weak, because life (understood as one's existence) as such, has no value in our currently dominant (neoliberal) language. If, in addition, 'difficult tenants' appear in the discourse, life turns into 'bare life'[22] and people into 'scum' who can be easily thrown out on the street.

As I wrote above, the paradox of absolutist freedom is on the one hand its detachment from a concrete man, and on the other a reduction to a codified choice. Absolute freedom is then devilish freedom (if we accept the Christian perspective of Satan as the prince of this world). It is located beyond man, but not beyond the world. It is an interesting experiment – on the one hand we have a man completely abstracted from the context (including the context of one's own body), on the other, a stable and orderly world, like a big supermarket shelf with different types of washing powder. We can only choose from what is available.

The freedom of creation is completely different. This is not freedom to choose, this is freedom of narration, the freedom that sets new territories and takes full responsibility for them. If, then, absolutist freedom binds an individual through choices set out by someone else, the freedom of creation allows one to present different versions of the story and invite others to the discussion. The freedom of creation is the freedom of an architect, who is subject to strict limitations (such as budget, client's preferences, legal regulations and finally the location) but can still present more than one version of the project. (The client's freedom of choice is then reduced to a choice between the presented versions.)

Freedom of creation is obviously connected with the responsibility of one's actions. In contrast to the freedom of choice, which restricts and enslaves man with values transcendent to him, the freedom of creation widens and opens the perspective of future changes and activities. Freedom of creation produces a surplus of being, whereas freedom of choice only changes the order of what already exists.

The second manipulated concept is property. In the liberal tradition, property constitutes man. It is man and only man who owns himself and is therefore entitled to possess things. This is a crucial notion, because if we assume that man owns himself, we get fixated on property and no radical change is possible. But can we really believe that man owns himself? After Freud, Lacan and Derrida? Of course, man doesn't own himself. Man creates and negotiates. To live means to participate in the work of creation, to continue describing, discovering and creating the world. Obviously, the liberal tradition descends from the biblical tradition, albeit having adapted the biblical creation of the world into its own story. The relationship between man and things is important because it concerns the relationship between inside and outside. It constitutes the inside in dialogue with the outside, blurring them both and creating hybrid narratives. Within these narratives new alliances can be born – between our taste and food, between place and our sense of smell and social conventions. These alliances, which constitute ourselves in various narratives, are not based on our possession of places and things but on their teetering and temporary relationships with us.

In the city, the key element of contemporary debate is the idea of place. This debate originates from the phenomenological tradition of Heidegger, Norbert-Schulz and Christopher Alexander, further developed by theorists such as Juhani Pallasmaa or Mark Auge[23]. At its core, however, this is

Heidegger's theory.

Place is different to space as there is a clear, emotional core of human behaviour in our human existence in the world. Place has an essential authenticity, the concept beloved by many architects as genius loci. The place is familiar and authentic – it belongs to us. Architecture, however, is the manipulation of archetypical forms (signs). This perspective in political practice combines perfectly with the concept of property (ownership) and merges into a single reactionist narrative of rooted residents versus nomads without a place and therefore without authentic attributes. In this narrative, residents are citizens, real people, whereas nomads are, at best, a source of cash (as tourists), knowledge (visiting experts) or cheap labour (immigrants). Most often, however, they are a threat, a possible pollutant. The phenomenological horizon of liberal inclusivity is the concept of integration, where visitors can become integrated with the local community. This is the most radical thought such attitudes can afford.

This of course comes from the vision of man as the integral whole, as if these 'rooted residents' didn't watch TV, had no friends in other cities and countries and didn't belong to any national or global groups and organisations. Instead of seeing them as a stable and integral group, why not try and see them as parts of a narrative where the individual characteristics of residents and nomads are intertwined? It has nothing to do with integration: on the contrary, it is a heterodox story, built on differences and the breakdown of the homogeneity of the subject.

Within post-Heidegger discourse today it is popular to connect uprooting (regarded as negative) with modernity. Marc Auge introduced the concept of non-place, which quickly became yet another fascination of architects and urbanists. (It is unsurprising, given the widespread belief that architects and planners are primarily involved in place making.) So what is a non-place? It is space that doesn't allow for emotional attachment, which is too banal, standard, and generally, serves as a transitory space between 'real' places. Non-places include the highway, a hotel room, an airport. These are also places where ownership is faceless, yet hold a strong panoptical control.

The negative reception to non-places derives from the Heideggerean binding of being with dwelling, as presented in the essay 'Building, dwelling, thinking'[24], compulsory reading in many architectural schools. If maliciously interpreted, dwelling could be understood as the existential appropriation of space. To be called 'place', a space needs to allow us to bond with it, and to explain it on a high note – a space through which we can reach transcendence. In contrast, non-place is a nihilistic void.

The second very influential concept in architecture is a simulacrum (but rather as understood by Baudrillard, not Deleuze). In keeping with para-theological language, a simulacrum is a lie, an unsuccessful and sometimes evil imitation of being created by the *demiurge*.

Almost everybody can tell the difference between a historical market place and a modern high-rise estate without difficulty. It would also be very easy to convince most people that the latter is a place without meaning, a non-place. Perhaps, for a tourist, a high-rise estate has far fewer significant elements: it is visually 'smooth' because it lacks easily identifiable signs and symbols (such as statues, urban furniture, but also global brands which codify mass imagination and which at first glance might become gateways leading beyond place to somewhere eternal, or at least significant).

But if we look at urban space not from the point of view of an abstract tourist, but from the point of view of an inhabitant of a particular area, then it is the market place that may hold less meaning than the space between the high-rises. Where, then, does the power of the market place come from? It comes from education, city guides and culture. The market place does not mean anything by itself; it was filled with meaning and not necessarily by its users. The space of the high-rise estate is subjected to negative media coverage, but it is still more susceptible to the interpretations of the users. 'Place' is then a kind of a symbolic violence. Non-place is free from this symbolic violence, but in Auge's view, it is also a strictly controlled space. The user is offered a vision that can be either accepted or rejected. Again, this is the freedom of choice from a selection of pre-prepared options. Narratives connecting the observers with space and artefacts allow for an infinitive number of possible relationships but this freedom requires an effort on our side, a certain openness and a void in space. After all, it is not a coincidence that post-industrial spaces are so popular with artists. They are not blank sheets of paper but within their existing narrative obvious cracks exist, allowing and enabling new interpretations.

The relationship between man and the world does not need to be based on appropriation. Property is static and one-dimensional. A relationship based on a constructed story is a completely different kind – it is both local and extraterritorial, it concerns the physical as well as the imagined. It accepts temporality. Nobody is privileged, nobody is marginalised. It lasts only as long it is capable of defending its position and winning over enough people. The freedom of narrative is the freedom of creation, the freedom of constant searching for – and the discovery of! – better, more inclusive and therefore more effective stories.

Public space doesn't exist
(and neither does private)

When reading this book in your room, what space are you in? And if you happen to be in a park, how is the air you are breathing now different to the air in your room? Who owns the space you take when you sit on the park bench? Where really is the line between public and private, and what or who determines it: is it arbitrarily decided by the government and planners or by your own body?

Maybe there is neither public nor private space any more. Maybe today this distinction is more useless than ever before; these days we deal with spatial hybrids. Without even touching the topic of new media and new ways of communicating (for now at least – I will return to it later), there are many examples where the boundary between physical space and the sphere of pure information has been blurred – the flash mob is but one of these instances – and there are many examples of blurred boundaries between the private and the public.

Let's be clear then – there is no public or private space any more. In Gianbattista Nolli's[25] times it was inspiring to use a form of binary code to depict space but today we need to be aware that we are dealing with overlapping fields of interests and influence which fluctuate in their density. Therefore, it is impossible to define public space on the grounds of property rights or availability. Property rights do not translate directly to how space is used – the way space is used is the main feature of space in the city. Availability is not limited to the two modes of available/unavailable. New questions arise: the space is available for whom? Under what conditions? When? And at what price?

The fundamental distinction between public and private space that is still employed today was developed in the 1970s by Oscar Newman, author of the famous book 'Defensible space'[26].

Newman introduced a division of space into three kinds. He placed semi-public space between public and private space (with time, semi-private space was added to this narrative). This space 'in-between' was key to Newman's thought. Private space, as the name suggests, is supervised by people who are in full control over it and can decide who may enter it, and who may not. In contrast, semi-public space was conceived as space monitored by the community. Finally, for Newman, public space was nobody's space – even if he didn't describe it as such, this understanding of public space was the result of the thinking introduced in his works.

Newman's theory was conservative; it referred to community, ownership, supervision and control. It was an interesting attempt to rebuild community through territoriality. It is astonishing though, that at the end of the twentieth century, anyone could believe that a return to pre-urban social structures could be successful. However, maybe it should not be so surprising. Since the beginning of the twenty-first century in Britain, Conservatives have been trying to do the same, only on a much larger scale. As we know, Newman's attempt failed – instead of communities exercising control over 'their' territory, we ended up with gated communities where control is imposed by hired companies, external to the community. The conservative fear of the crowd lead to locked-down communities, secured in their own prisons with their own privately-hired guards.

This degeneration of the defensible space idea points to two important issues. Firstly, the relationship between space and a strictly defined community is questionable in the modern city, and secondly – also due to the blurring of the concept of community – it is impossible today to escape from external institutions and rely only on internal relationships built organically by people. In the context of the modern city, an organically-organised society needs hard, authoritarian control structures sooner or later.

The division into public and private space, or more generally, to the private and public realm, is still deeply rooted in our vision of the city. Richard Sennett in his book 'The Conscience of the Eye: The Design and Social Life of Cities'[27] defines the city as a kind of 'machine that separates' our privacy from the public realm. He blames this division on Christian theology, although his citation of Saint Augustine in this context rather indicates a Manichean trail.

So, the question arises: is the distinction between the private and the public actually such a curse? And in the context of our discussion – what then lies between the private and the public?

Oscar Newman attempted to answer this question, situating community between the individual and the mass[28]. To some extent it is close to Martin Buber's thought and his vision of the community as built on the relationship I–Thou. Harvey Cox points to the inadequacy of this theory when applied to the modern city. Cox is a radical theologian, an advocate of secularism, which he understands as the ultimate liberation of man from paganism and transition of the individual into a real, mature disciple of Jesus. His rejection of the communitarian vision of the city, in the sense of pre-urban social structures based on strong interpersonal bonds, is still relevant after 50 years, however controversial.

The problem with Cox's theses lies in the fact that by rejecting community (which is of course sometimes oppressive and of pre-urban origin) we remain in the vacuum between our individuality and human mass. Unfortunately, along with us, this vacuum contains institutions and organizations. They fill the vacuum and make it *de facto* cease to exist. Analysis of Cox's thought allows us to understand the degeneration of Newman's idea but it still doesn't allow us to understand if the question of the private–public division is still relevant.

Or maybe not: Cox is a liberal, and liberal thought maintains that the individual designates an absolute horizon of his thought. But if we look at the individual from a post-postmodern perspective, and are therefore aware that the subject is not a homogeneous whole (yet at the same time it doesn't disappear), then the question of liberation in the city and the role of the space between the private and public realm will take on new meaning. If the subject exists as a heterogeneous and wobbly structure we come back to the question of gaps between its elements and the nature of the relationship between these gaps[29] and the outside. Perhaps then, these gaps are what a subject uses to connect with everything that it is not? If so, then there is no distinction between private (subjective, individual) and public (external, contextual, collective) space, but only a division of space into interaction/collaboration and (through the void existing inside and outside of the subject) intimate space, which is constructed as self-conscious identities of the subject. It is important to note that intimacy is by no means synonymous with privacy. The notion of intimacy doesn't enjoy much respect from contemporary thinkers and the legacy of Freud and Lacan means it is something highly suspicious. We will avoid this dangerous territory and define it differently.

Dangers to privacy are highlighted, for example, when we talk about being filmed by CCTV. We seem to feel that if someone is filming us then our privacy is threatened, a little bit like mythical Indians believing that photographic portraits would steal a piece of their soul. And yet CCTV only multiplies what exists without technology: our presence (even potential) amongst others. By being in a space of cooperation we acquiesce to interaction. Again, however, we should negotiate the conditions of these interactions. This has nothing to do with privacy as intimacy is the lack of influence and a refusal to interact. Intimacy concerns not only individuals; it exists wherever there is an autarchy of relationship. A meeting of lovers is intimate, but not necessarily the meeting of a married couple.

But let us think about intimacy differently. Let us start with the classic ideas of inveteracy and homelessness, understood as an un-rooting from the natural world and consequently, the culture. Homelessness and the process of uprooting is continuous and impossible to stop. From this notion of traditionally understood homelessness (here we are referring to Heidegger, and Novalis, whom he cited) alienation is accelerated, and finally, we will find ourselves in a world where man is almost perfectly alone. Homelessness is then the fundamental trauma of human existence. In architecture's phenomenological tradition (drawing on Heidegger and developed by Christian Norberg-Schulz[30]) homelessness is linked with the loss of connection with place (see the persistent use of the concept of *genius loci* by Norberg-Schulz). However, this is not the only interpretation. The severed continuity with the world, and the resulting gap and void between the world and the subject, are existential experiences which should not be reduced to the loss of ties with a territory. Such a simplification leads to conservative, anti-nomadic obsession which, as in the case of Heidegger himself, a one-time member of Nazi party, can easily be interpreted as anti-Semitism[31].

A completely different view on homelessness is offered by Paolo Virno, a member of the Italian post-Marxist group of philosophers known as *Potere Operaio*. In his view, homelessness is an experience shared by all people and it provides a base upon which to build a community. Virno doesn't want to overcome homelessness – he wants to build on it. But he sees man as permanently alienated and disconnected from the world and nature.

This state of alienation and disconnection is not entirely valid. We exist in a continual process of detachment and reattachment to the world. The process of attachment to the world (plug-in) covers every aspect of human existence, including physical movement in space. With every single step we have to negotiate our position in an ever-changing environment, but it is not only about the relationship between the human body and its location in space: it is about identities of subject formed and adopted in the context of external conditions and circumstances. When at school we are teachers and pupils, when at a restaurant we are waiters and clients. Our identities are constructed through language that is within and beyond us, through our own hormones and alien, external food and drink. They are always identities, not one identity. What reveals them and weaves them together is the context, the exterior, the world.

It is impossible for an individual to stay mentally healthy without external stimuli, as experiments with sensory deprivation[32] prove. This is because the world provides consistency and continuity of human consciousness – man cannot exist without the world. Therefore to defend the notion of intimacy is not the same as cutting man off from the world. The division between intimacy and cooperation is different to the division between private and public.

Intimate space is a space of free exploration of a single identity – in such space we might be sitting in an armchair, on a bench in the park with a book or taking a stroll in the woods. In contrast, the space of interaction is the space in which we move from one identity to another and present multiple identities simultaneously. When I work in a restaurant as a waiter it is because I perform a function defined in relation to others. In addition to being a waiter I am also a colleague and a father working to provide for his children. To simplify, the intimate space is a space for us, the individual, whereas the space of interaction is a space for others and the individual as formed through others.

In the space of interaction we are constantly changing our identity. We oscillate between being for ourselves and being for others. This oscillation makes the idea of ownership or stable functions as designated to space seem if not absurd then insufficient at best. This constant plugging in and out makes the interface, the language of surface, the most important concept we are going to use. It doesn't matter then what is happening beneath the surface, in the depth, which is understood here as a self-conscious identity and not as a Jungean subconsciousness. In fact – we shouldn't be interested in this at all! The outer skin, the surface reacting to other surfaces: this is important. These surfaces are like semi-permeable membranes, produced in a continuous process of identities morphing into one another. It is this (re)active nature of the surface which is crucial to our further considerations.

The division of space into interaction/collaboration and intimate space has an obvious impact on how we perceive the city and architecture, as well as how we think architecture and cities should be formed. It is necessary to ensure that space exists where this flow of space between intimacy and interaction can occur and where multiple identities can interact.

Most of the emerging so-called public spaces keep their users in a limbo of indeterminacy. These spaces do not allow for intimacy and neither do they invite interaction. An empty square with a solitary bench (and a pay-to-use toilet nearby) is arguably worse than even one of the widely-criticised shopping malls. The problem with these malls is only partially spatial. What they do is reduce users to mere consumers. They objectify people not only as they look at goods, but also as they see other users as objects on display. The spatial isolation of the mall from the city cuts off its users from other, non-consumerist logics.

It is possible to correct these aspects of shopping malls. Problems of another, more critical kind, those relating to taxes, working conditions and other regulations, will become obvious and demand to be resolved when we stop seeing 'evil' shopping malls in opposition to 'good' squares with benches. The discussion about shopping malls disguising themselves as public space is pointless and leads us nowhere. Public space doesn't exist and there is no point in talking about it anymore.

Space of direct action

Whatever happens, whenever we take action, there is a gap between the planning and preparation phase and the actual action. In our world, where many are convinced that a butterfly in Kuala Lumpur can cause a storm in New York, it is important to remind oneself of this basic fact. The ease with which we connect everything to everything leads us to believe that whatever we do, it is real action, and even if it can't be seen here and now, our butterfly movements will eventually cause a storm somewhere, eventually. It is obviously a comforting thought but unfortunately it's not true: most of our actions are just background noise – they will never become melodies.

Real action is always the result of plexus: something has to weave with something else for a – even temporarily – stable node. A series of weak, individually insignificant events create a coalition, a plexus, a weave, a structure. Obviously, how individual elements, actors and actions associate with each other is crucial. It doesn't mean, however, that there is no difference between categories of being[33]. This difference manifests itself primarily on the surface, in the 'interface' that structures use to plug into each other. Therefore, one can suggest that the city is formed on the surface where consumption and production of goods and services is revealed. On these surfaces and between them, this is where the city forms itself as a being which is more than a sum of its subsystems. Here we must clearly distinguish between interfaces/surfaces and the void/space between them. What does function as a medium in the city? What fills the void? What is the medium in the city? Perhaps, instead of treating void as another absolute (but not excluding this point of view), it is enough if we define it as a lack of an element, a missing bit. It is intuitively easier to imagine the world as not homogenous. If then, there is a difference between 'this' and 'that', 'me' and 'you', even if there is something in this distinction, what is missing is more important.

Henri Bergson wrote that 'the representation of emptiness is always full' and today Manuel De Landa proposes a magma which floods all holes and cracks[34]. Our contemporary imagination does not help: it is very hard to imagine void, which is really empty, without fields, waves and particles of matter. Instead of naturalistic metaphors it may be worth (at least for a moment) going in a different direction. The best guide – but a lazy one, as he shows us the direction but never goes there himself – is Emile Cioran, who said: "The danger lies in treating the void as a substitute for being which would invalidate the basic function of the void which is sabotaging the mechanisms of attachment."[35]

It is not what void is, but what it does – this is what is crucial in this definition. If flat ontology sees the world as a continuum, where everything is linked with each other, then void is the only barrier against an all encompassing determinism. Void breaks the sequence of cause and effect and gives us freedom; freedom needed for change and development.

The metaphor of void can be embedded in different languages. It can be a language of geometry, seeing void as distance, or history, which sees void as interval. Cioran's void is derived from the language of history but these two languages – spatial and temporal – are complementary when we consider the city, which is after all the time-space being.

Cioran himself frequently wrote about the city, often manifesting his aversion to the city: "Whenever I happen to be in a city of any size, I marvel that riots do not break out everyday: Massacres, unspeakable carnage, a doomsday chaos. How can so many human beings coexist in a space so confined without hating each other to death?"[36] He responds to this question in a fashion typical of him – the answer is that people do hate each other, but they are too weak and bland to bring themselves to fury and killing. We, however, will go another way and will not search for answers to the question as to why people do not massacre each other in cities (especially since we know cases when they do). Instead we will ask a basic question: what makes people coexist in the city and therefore – what really does constitute the city?

The romantic view of the city, extremely popular today, dates back to the words of Shakespeare: "What is the city but the people?"[37] In fact this viewpoint reduces the city simply to people, and its functioning to meetings and conversations. This vision of the city as a large agora, and of public space as a cross between a discussion club and a meat market, is naïve and dangerous. Not because these visions are untrue but precisely because they somehow manage to touch the essence of the city.

From this point of view, any city is in essence just a small town. It attempts to transfer the archetype of the Greek Polis or any small town, let it be Bon Temps, Louisiana or Twin Peaks, Washington into the reality of global cities. This is a pre-urban sentiment which sometimes refers to Buber's relationship of I-Thou. However, in a big city, this kind of intimate relationship is extremely difficult and attempting to achieve it leads only to frustration and in turn to anti-urban phobia.

So – if not a direct relationship of I-Thou – then what? To answer, I will not refer to superficial relationships which we establish in the city – an exchange of smiles with a shop assistant or 'thank you' to the bus driver. These are nice moments but they do not constitute the city, they do not build any structure. The city exists through institutions. As I wrote in one of my essays:

When I was younger I loved books by Phillip K. Dick. It is an important introduction because it explains why a Coca-Cola can speaking with God's voice wouldn't appear as something really special to me. This time, however, there was no can and nobody talked to me. It was a sunny morning in London, and my daughter and I left our provincial Plymouth to see a 'real' city. My daughter, seduced by the familiar logo, proposed a breakfast in Starbucks. Two coffees, sandwiches and a muffin. At a table next to us, an elderly couple enjoyed two coffees, sandwiches and a muffin. And then I understood.

Contemporary debate on public space in the city is contaminated by Habermas' idea of the public sphere and a change in the language of modern philosophy. When we talk about public spaces we refer primarily to places where people can meet and talk to each other. These face to face meetings are seen as the essence of the city. Nothing could be further from the truth.

Even the most active among us are unable to get to know more people by name and surname than a couple of hundred of fellow citizens, and even collecting 'friends' on Facebook doesn't help. In ancient Greece the debate concerning the optimum number of city inhabitants fluctuated around ten thousand people (for example, for Plato this figure was 5040 adult men). It is not possible for cities inhabited by hundreds of thousands and very often millions of people to be fundamentally bound by dialogical face-to-face relationships. If the city is not a place for meeting, not a place for conversation, then what?

My epiphany in Starbucks didn't concern the transcendent importance of coffee, sandwiches or muffins. It concerned what united the couple sitting at a nearby table with my daughter and I. It wasn't a face-to-face meeting or a conversation (which would probably never have happened). It was the organisation, transcendent to all of us, which in this case was the corporation of Starbucks. It was there, during production, marketing and logistics, where the medium that united these strangers had been produced. It is through institutions (very loosely defined) that we exist as a society and it is through various institutions that the city exists. The city is not people but institutions and non-human mechanisms. Fortunately for us we are still the essential parts of these...

Obviously, this is a major simplification because this is not an institution, even a social institution as such, that we discuss here. It is more about two consonant mechanisms.

On one hand, this is about an 'external view', about the idea of community that derives from the writings of Sartre: a community that is created through being transcendent to the I-Thou relationship, the discipling and discipled community. The city is viewed as a giant Panopticon, albeit a very specific one. This Panopticon doesn't interfere with privacy and comes to life only when two or three – or a crowd – gather. It is a Panopticon acting towards what is public, not what is individual and intimate, the one not serving the control of citizens but rather building and reinforcing social binds.

On the other hand, it is about the mechanism/structure which treats people only as a resource. In the above essay I wrote about a cafe, in which people of course work and to which customers come for a coffee and cake, but both work and consumption can be codified: in these situations we don't have to deal with fully dimensional people with all their richness and complexity, but only with creatures defined by functions they perform. Institutions reduce people to a set of procedures.

The mechanism of the formation of structures external to man, which then in turn organise his actions and behaviour, is in fact a description of the formation of society, civilization and culture. In my previous book[38] I referred to the writings of Pierre Manent, who stated that from the Middle Ages until the end of the 19th century, the city along with empire, nation-state and church, was one of the fundamental political ideas of the Western civilization. Each of these ideas shapes the society according to the joint cultural framework. However, the city is an exception to this. For this reason Manent considered the idea of the city as weak, unable to resist the strong ideas of empire and church. We also know that the city is weaker than the nation-state. This is an interesting distinction; on one hand there is a heterogeneous Empire based on strong ideological and institutional but not ethnic foundations. On the other hand, we have the nation-state, which includes whatever holds Empire together but also adds ethnic identity, which as we know is an extremely strong and effective binder. Obviously, the city can be based on one ethnic group, but usually – and especially when we consider contemporary cities – they are mixtures of various religions, ethnicities and languages. However, this diversity is not the real weakness of the city but – as in the case of the nation-state – it is the loss of subjectivity and power as it trickles away to global markets and organisations. The weakness of today's city is related to its identity crisis. Not only is it difficult to imagine a modern city based on strong ideological foundations, but it is also doubtful that urban society itself exists. How, then, is this 'external eye' formed and how do the structures external to the individual shape human behaviour? Indeed, in one way the city liberates people from pre-urban conditions and binds, but in another it hinders its inhabitants in a million new ways. Perhaps we should embrace multitude, not community. This is the multitude as introduced by Leibniz and today used by Hardt, Negri and Paolo Virno[39].

To define the city as a natural, physical emanation of the multitude may look intriguing at first glance, but soon serious doubts arise. First of all, the sense of alienation on which the multitude is based is hardly a state in which anything other than a momentary outburst of resentment could happen. Usually, alienation is considered a pathology, a condition which must be escaped. This is what happens – instead of a single universal common ground, we use many ethnic, religious or ideological dens for shelter. The universalism of the multitude shatters into a million languages and cultural codes. However, in a way, Virno is correct to look for social bonds other than ethnic or cultural ones. There is some kind of mysterious connection between people in the city and somehow the city functions. How this connection is constructed and what it really is – these are the questions I want to ask.

If the city actually works and some kinds of bonds between people exist, then the question is: Are these bonds transcendent to the people? Or maybe on the contrary: are they constructed by people themselves, within the I-Thou relationship?

First of all, we should probably reject simplistic dichotomies and start looking for answers in a more sophisticated way. Let the word 'interface' be a clue for us – interface as in what is in between, what belongs and doesn't belong at the same time. Of course, I realise that this word brings about mechanistic associations and it is impossible to escape them completely. Nevertheless, the potential of this word is well worth using.

There is a temptation to start defining interfaces with analogies we are familiar with. It can be said that interfaces rely on institutions, organisations and conventions. Another approximation would be the attempt to describe how interfaces work. A tripartite division of interfaces could be used for that: intimate, internal and external. Intimate interface would be described as based on the I-Thou relationship, open to change and constructed during the process of communication by partners taking part. Obviously, there is always a starting point and negotiation, and the construction of the interface doesn't begin ex nihilo. However, the process itself is not limited by anything except for its effectiveness as evaluated by its users/constructors. At the beginning, when two people meet, they behave and speak according to the convention they are used to. For example, if this is a church choir meeting it is highly unlikely for them to start the conversation with questions about the latest episode of a risqué TV series, and if at the pub, it is usually safe to start a conversation on the last performance of the local football team. A ready-made template is employed when dealing with strangers. Only after some time into the relationship is the convention tweaked and further defined by the people involved.

Conventions can be considered – in a very simplified way – as examples of intimate interfaces. This kind of interface describes a slow process of building of a 'common language' by people who are in a very close, intimate (but not necessarily sexual) relationship. Wittgenstein was obviously right in his statements that there is no private language (although there is always the question of how we communicate with ourselves...). Intimate interface is its closest approximation. Its use is obviously limited, and yet discussion of it is worthwhile because of the mechanism of its construction, over which we have at least some control. If we understand where this interface comes from, and where its limitations lie, it will be easier to understand the next level of this typology.

The second type is the internal interface with its own set of rules (a basic cultural framework), partly open to bottom-up changes, but also strongly influencing the people who use it. While this may lead us astray, we can begin to imagine what such an interface is and to think about it as a kind of organisation. It is possible to negotiate the rules of use for this interface but they are subject to considerable inertia. However, its most significant part is the ties between the users and the medium. This interface is active in choosing which users are accepted and which rejected, and furthermore it imposes certain behaviour, forms and educates its users. Our influence over this interface is more limited than in the previous case and this is where we fully start to feel external social pressure, existing outside our subjectivity.

Finally, the most transcendent / independent interface to the user is the external interface in which bottom-up changes are almost impossible. However, contrary to the internal interface it doesn't try to form its users, rather allowing them to plug in and out at will. It is not neutral, but it is almost perfectly trans-cendent. Trivializing, it can be said that any kind of institution is this interface. It is worth stopping here at the example of the Catholic Church – still a very effective institution today, despite its structure being dramatically different from what is generally considered effective at the beginning of the 21st century (social networks, for example).

Our tripartite typology, however appealing, is rather dangerous and simply ineffective. It is because between these three types, there is an almost unlimited number of intermediate possibilities and hybrids. None of these models will ever occur in pure form. However, the aforementioned language, being above all the external interface – shapes us (the internal interface) and also, under specific circumstances we create our private languages (the intimate interface). Especially today, when technology (internet, mobile phones) so radically affects social life, these three types of interfaces should be treated more as a starting point, rather than a finite and closed model.

This is a moment to excuse our use of technological language to describe social relations – this is simply because humanity as we knew it doesn't exist anymore. We have entered a post-human phase without even noticing how cyborg we have become. There is no need to be ashamed or to try and deny it. But it means that instead of simplifying the idea of the interface to three types only, it is probably better to write it down as an open definition, focusing on its essence. What are these interfaces then?

First of all, the interface 'works', not 'is'. It reveals itself in action, not in contemplation. The status of the interface is dialec-tical: on one hand, it touches the subject / actor partially, but it never absorbs it whole. On the other hand, the interface obviously exceeds the subject / actor. It is then external to the subject whilst at the same time allowing it to actualise and act. Without the interface, the subject becomes solipsistic.

The most interesting feature of the interface is what is lacking and void. Interface is composed from external concepts previously internalised by the subject (and in principle plural subjects, as the interface cannot exist with a single subject). There is a gap between the concept internalised by the subject and the concept as a part of the interface – these concepts are not the same, only similar. There are similar gaps between various concepts delivered by different subjects, within the interface. Every gap, every void, must be overcome in the process of using the interface. The effectiveness of the interface requires for the gaps to be almost imperceptible and the effort needed to overcome them as small as possible. When the interface works with almost perfect efficiency, it simply means that a functional fragment was internalised by the actors using the interface. Since the interface shapes the functioning subject, it is very difficult to see the difference, and moreover, a gap is treated as an obstacle. The interface forces users to adopt their own logic to minimise the gaps.

Freedom and the free will of users is located in gaps within the interface. Wherever there is a possibility of negotiation (as in the case of the intimate interface), on the one hand the efficiency of the interface is reduced but on the other an opportunity for innovation arises. It is worth remembering that innovation doesn't necessary mean a solution which upgrades the functioning of the capitalist system – it can also have a revolutionary character.

The description of the operation of the interface draws our attention to the existence of gaps and voids overcome by its users. This is a fundamental issue! If we assume that individual beings (social and otherwise) do not completely adhere to each other, that there is no magma – a universal medium tying them together – so when we agree that in fact there are gaps and cracks between them, that there is emptiness separating this from that, me from you, then the interface is a structure constructed from surfaces only. The interface is constructed from arbitrarily chosen ends 'of the same', ends of certain specific identities. The interface is then like a spatial being constructed from perfectly flat surfaces. The spaces 'in between' are spaces of action.

The inclusive but undemocratic city?

In the Polish city of Łódź, there used to operate (and some people claim it still does) The Group of Certain People, an informal network of urban activists. It was a group with a nearly perfectly anarchic, egalitarian structure of management: it is difficult to speak of any leadership, or even about a structure that could be described as democratic. The Group of Certain People acted more like a cloud of potentials, in which every so often, a few – sometimes a dozen or several dozen – people condensed around an idea. This condensation led to action. There was no debate or voting but almost chaotic eruptions of stored energy.

At first glance, it may be concluded that The Group of Certain People (GCP) is a free, almost organically emerging structure, an unstable structure-assemblage[40]. But is it really? What if we see GCP as an extremely disciplined, almost authoritarian sect? However provocative it sounds, let us try – at least for a moment and as an experiment – to see it in this way. First of all, to enter the cloud of GCP, you need to adopt a certain set of values as your own. This is the first test, the first step of selection. However, if GCP really was a cloud of potentials then anyone could be a part of it. This is to some extent common to any organisation we consider, and it is important to emphasise that GCP is not an exception to this, however strongly we might wish it was.

When you pass the test of shared values – or at least you share the interest in the city at the outset – the process of testing doesn't stop, because every idea is tested by the group. If your idea wins the group's support, the action takes place, and if not, the idea dies a natural death.

It is an almost perfect resemblance of the modern consumer market where in order for a product to be successful, it needs to gain support – it must be desired and bought by a certain number of consumers. It doesn't necessary have to be the largest group, however; even if the majority considers the product to be inferior, it doesn't affect the commercial success of the product unless its sale is blocked for legal reasons. If a product or a concept has a loyal audience, a niche, it remains on the market. Obviously, neither the structure of the operation of the GCP nor the consumer market is democratic in any traditional understanding. However, what is interesting and important is that both the consumer market and the structure of GCP resembles the structure of the city, its neighbourhoods, separated fragments with overlapping incompatible orders. This structure – although it is not democratic – is not necessarily oppressive and exclusive. The city is not homogeneous despite the legal system. In fact, the regulations for individual parts are different.

These differences can arise from the progressing privatization of urban space, as responsibility for fragments of urban space is taken over by various organizations and companies. It can also be related to differences in conventions recognized by various communities in the multi-ethnic and multicultural city. (There are different norms for Catholics, Protestants, Hindu, Muslims, etc.)

Here we are reaching a very important question: is this diversity in culture and identity desirable? It is a sensitive issue which cannot be solved using black and white criteria. On one hand, it is difficult to question the right of different groups to define their unique identity as it would be for the individual. On the other hand, however – if in the city we meet 'no longer Jew or Greek'[41], does it mean that those pre-urban identities should disappear? However, even if they do, the division for inhabitants of districts A and B still remains.

The solution is to challenge dualistic thinking, not to replace it with Latourian thinking about relationships, but rather by blurring them and including the differences between subjects (as we know from Hegel, to speak about the difference is to speak about similarity, subjects themselves and finally relationships ("the Other"))[42]. Instead of thinking yes – no, I -You, we need to think yes – perhaps yes – maybe – not necessarily – no. I – You – We – Them – Us and Them – I and You, I – it – You.

This does not mean we reject being a Jew or a Greek. Instead, we are simply adding the identity of being a resident of the city. Identities remain, but rather accumulate and layer, grow through each other, fertilising each other and undergoing hybridization. But this is not enough – it is barely a description of what exists. It is a statement that many may find easy to agree with, and at first glance it appears typically postmodern. However, this is not the alternative we are searching for. We are closer to the ontology proposed by Alain Badiou, which sees in every situation a surplus element not subjected to representation[43]. We are not – and I hope to be forgiven for this simplification – in a position to propose such an individual description without reducing reality, which itself is always a multiplicity. This surplus, this excess, allows us to question anew the existing description/represen-tation and make another attempt at a better, more complete description. The fact that reality will always elude us and the description will never fully correspond with it should not disco-urage us. On the contrary: as Too-ticky[44] would say, "All things are so very uncertain, and that's exactly what makes me feel reassured."

If, however, we leave Badiou here and come back to the city, there still remains the question – what is between different identities? Or rather – how does the transition from one identity to another occur? To take one individual, how does a shift occur from the identity of a Greek, to an inhabitant of a district A, later to a husband and finally to a member of the Seashell Collectors Club? What causes (enables?) the transitions between these identities?

The answer is obvious: the external context and internal features of the subject are actualised in a specific identity. It is the discontinuity of the subject, the fact that between its (potential) identities/characteristics there is void, enabling them to reveal themselves. This is not the 'either – or' situation but 'this and that' in a given situation. Determination of a single identity doesn't negate others, however it actualises and implements itself in a given narrative. But the key feature of this narrative is its universality – once it is disclosed, it tries to cover everything and make everything a part of itself. Contrary to the logic of GCP or the consumer market, which is satisfied with a fragment, universal narrative is total but not totalitarian[45]. However, thinking about the city within the universal narrative is different to thinking within a mechanistic democracy in which people are reduced to their votes. What is then this universal narrative and how does it relate to the previously used examples of partial narratives: GCP, consumer market and the city?

Both partial and universal narrative is possible due to the existence of the structure transcendent to subjects/actors. For GCP it was its set of rules and conventions, for the consumer market it is primarily money and for the city it is the administration and legal system (but also the physical elements of its structure – buildings, roads, infrastructure, etc.).

Every time then, when we speak about the partial narrative, it is only possible because there is a universal meta-narrative which enables the actualising of diversities.

Between different orders in which we operate – being in a relationship, in a family, a group of friends or at work – there are gaps, which we would rather we didn't see. It is easier to assume continuity, to assume that a man is a medium himself in which all these different orders are joined/merged. This is true, except the man himself is constructed around the void.

If this wasn't the case, would a translation from one order to the other be at all necessary? Is the fact that these different orders still exist – even if we pretend they don't – the evidence that the gaps between them do exist? And if the void exists, then doesn't the question of how it is overcome become the most important? How do two people communicate through the abyss of the void/emptiness?

A closer look at the structure of the GCP and the consumer market leads to another important conclusion: these are not uncoordinated and chaotic activities. Obviously, an element of emergence exists in them both, but it operates within the previously outlined framework. Like Rem Koolhaas in Lagos[46], the person who can't see these networks isn't looking carefully enough. So entranced by the informal economy of the city, he ignored incredibly strong and stable hierarchical structures. These political and clan structures are corrupt to the core and they bind this supposedly 'self-organizing' society.

These invisible structures can be described as the interfaces as mentioned in the previous chapter. Two key aspects of interfaces are firstly the breaking of the continuity of being, and secondly, the oscillation between outside and inside, which allows for interpersonal interactions to occur. It is a cliché that we never communicate directly, but the banality of this fact makes it too often ignored.

Juxtaposing the idea of interface with the city, we need first to address the idea of public space in the form it takes in contemporary architectural and urban discourse. It is usually defined as a primitive materialisation of Habermas' public sphere. I will come back to the idea of empty space in the city; for now I would like to point out that it is not the public sphere, but the concept of general intellect that seems to be a far more interesting trope to be followed when creating and analysing public space in the city. General intellect, briefly mentioned by Karl Marx in Grundrisse, concerns the process of growth of the importance of knowledge in the production process and the process of capitalisation of that knowledge.

Every machine, whether an engine or a computer, contains frozen knowledge, technical expertise and also general knowledge (for example language) – which theoretically belongs to everybody. Today, general intellect has become the central motive for Marxist philosophers referring to the Italian movement Potere Operaio (a part of Marxist autonomists)[47]. It is based mainly on the idea of human bodies becoming more and more cyborg-like as means of production. It concerns creative industries or to put it more generally – knowledge based enterprises – where a scientist, a programmer or a designer creates the product. As I mentioned before, the process of *cyborgisation* also affects society – people as a collective. There is no doubt then, that not only machines and bodies but also the space itself – as a social construct – contains general intellect. Aforementioned interfaces also become machines for coding and decoding information and knowledge. Interfaces as coders and decoders are becoming the most important elements of the capitalistic machinery.

How can these considerations be applied to the city? And how does void fit into all this?

Public space, besides being a vulgar version of Habermas's public sphere, is also a banalised emptiness. It was Lefebvre[48] who wrote about the rhythm of the city and about the full/empty opposition. The space between buildings has always fascinated urbanists and what until recently was considered empty. This was until postmodern thinkers, such as Lefevbre and Doreen Masey, filled it with meanings and it became a social construct. The emptiness disappeared. Instead, an all-encompassing magma appeared. I am not sure whether we realise what this means. The magma, as it glues together all the particles of being, prevents any change. It is not possible to imagine a post-capitalist world, because there is nothing but capitalism. There is no pause, there is not a moment of hesitation between steps. There is only continuity, the omnipresent and all-encompassing slush gluing and connecting everything together. One order, one idea, one goal. To the sounds of postmodern marches we happily entered the prison of liquid totalitarianism.

There is no escape from it because it is impossible to break what is liquid. What can be done then? What is liquid has to be frozen, merged and then divided. Only what is solid can be broken. Is it possible then, that adopting conservative thinking about the city is the most revolutionary, progressive and radical stance yet?

As Cioran wrote, void blocks totalitarian homogenisation. But that's not all: void is something more important, requiring a decision and will to overcome it. Heroic will. However, this will to make decisions assumes that we are free, that we can get out of the determinism of the flat ontology and jump over the abyss of non-being at will. Void doesn't homogenise, on the contrary – it means that what is broken can be put back together, and that what had never been can be built. If underneath the matter lies void, everything is still possible. Void gives us hope. It enables the existence of interfaces – various identities reveals themselves thanks to it. These interfaces contain this void within them. Interfaces are both inside and outside us, they allow us to be plugged in and to plug in. They contain passivity and they assume an act of will.

Partial, fragmented activity, as in the models of the GCP, the consumer market and the city, is a useful reminder that inclusive and undemocratic structures are simultaneously possible. However, they only exist if based on universal meta-structures. The difference between reformism and revolution lies in the attitude towards the meta-structures. Reformism does not challenge them; it only tries to work out which local substructures are communicating with the meta-structure. An example of this action is taxing capital flow and introducing local currencies. Revolution has a more radical goal – to replace one metastructure with another. Time banks are a good example because, despite being local and partial solutions, they have revolutionary potential because they propose a narrative different to capitalism. Both reformism and revolution are possible thanks to the non-homogeneous structure of being, mainly in a social dimension. The basic task for all who are joined in disagreement to the world as it is now is to keep this heterogeneity alive. It is not a coincidence that pluralism was such a popular word during the fall of the real socialism and emergent capitalism in Eastern Europe. In addition, the fact that this word almost completely fell from use is one proof of the growing homogeneity and totalitarian danger of the meta-narrative in which we live today. Today's fundamental task is to bring back the importance of this word, pluralism.

Constructed space, constructed by space

In Poland, architects and urban planners are amongst the professions which see themselves as depositaries of the universal 'common good' (at least with regards to urban space). At the 2008 Congress of Polish Architecture, one of the discussion panels explored the relationship between space and citizens and in the materials provided for discussion, the following statement was made:

> *Democracy: the equal participation of citizens (society) in the exercise of power. These are rights but also duties, and participation in management of space is one of these. To administer space and the protection of its resources is an important demonstration of caring for the common good.*

While this may not seem important, I think it is worth looking at the way in which Polish architects understand democracy and relationships between political power, citizens and experts (including themselves within that latter group).

Let us start with 'Democracy – it is the equal participation of citizens (society) in the exercise of power (...)'. Are there only citizens in the city? Obviously not, and one European example that comes to mind is Riga where – as recently as 2009 – thirty per cent of inhabitants didn't hold Latvian citizenship. This also concerns any other city that attracts immigrants whose legal status is not regulated. The problem, however, is not only political. In every city there is a substantial and growing percentage of people who are residents but not citizens: tourists and seasonal workers alongside high-earning and influential experts, as well as children and young people who have a big impact on the cities that they live in. The next excerpt, setting democracy in the context of 'participation in management of space', seems to be overly narrowing the problem. Democracy, participation and management are notions which have to be very carefully defined before they can be used in one sentence. Participation doesn't preclude hierarchic subordination and management doesn't imply democracy. These semantic considerations are not facetious exercises because they are closely linked with important questions about the positions of inhabitants, city officials and experts (architects, planners and others). These questions in turn are linked closely with the next excerpt from the declaration concerning the common good.

I must admit that the phrase 'concern for the common good' makes me very suspicious. It is because I always ask myself: Who decides what this common good is, and why are they always architects and planners together with politicians? It seems that this phrase is generally used by powerful people who intend to morally blackmail less powerful local communities, yet demand respect for their personal or professional interests. The common good then becomes a tool in establishing hegemony rather than the universal idyll it is often presented as.

Besides the instrumental use of the 'common good' phrase by planners, architects, officials and politicians, and even assuming their good will, there is still cause for concern. The fact that the term is used signifies the positivist approach to planning and the city. The common good – even from this idealistic perspective – is in fact presented as something objectively existing and therefore something to be recognised and implemented. It can only be recognised by appropriately prepared people – either through education (architects and planners) or because of the high position they hold, allowing them to see the world from an almost divine perspective. It is the moment of arrogance which in fact reduces the importance of democracy and 'people power', assuming that decisions should only be made by these who claim to understand the city. This is where democracy collapses when confronted with the common good[49]. Instead of the mutilated

democracy I would like to discuss power as in the archaic understanding of planners, where power is something to be possessed.
But what kind of power? There are at least two kinds of power to
be distinguished.

There is a negative power – the power of restrictions and
regulations, the power that prevents something from happening;
and there is a causal power – the one that enables change,
activity and the sole fact of *happening*. In the neoliberal regime
the latter is privileged in relation to the former. The negative
power has to be reduced so the causal power can flourish. The
type of power that planners and officials have is negative power.
It is also important to note that this conflation of planners with
officials is very significant, and I am not sure that even the
planners and officials themselves are fully aware of its consequences. A planner becomes a passive function, acting as a
guardian of the sacred flame of the common good. However, the
planner is fundamentally separated from those who really need
what he is guarding: they don't need the sacred flame, they need
something they can cook on. Obviously, I am not trying to
defend petrified institutions but neither am I going to condemn
them unconditionally. The problematic relationship between
what is alive and changing and what tries to organise life is
indeed as old as the civilization itself.

It seems to me that the definition of the institution as being in
opposition to life and change is a mistake. The institution doesn't
negate life; it elevates it to the next level. The institution is not
intended to conserve the present – it allows for an effective
complication which cannot be achieved by individual people.
Simply, the institution can do more. In this narrative the planner
and the official are not the guardians of the sacred flame any
more; instead they become teachers and innovators. It is not their
goal to protect what is dead but to support what is alive. The
recently celebrated successes of the South American cities of
Porto Alegre, Curitiba and Bogota are narratives of power which

ceased guarding and started creating. Contrary to the neoliberal myth, power in these cities didn't disappear. Just the opposite: it is strong and effective. Let's return for a moment to the two kinds of power which I mentioned above.

Both types of power are stable in their own way. The negative power is obviously less mobile, but every power 'moves', its presence is temporary rather than continuous. Power is constructed between actors/players, it is not assigned to any of them for good. In fact, all major contemporary urban theories – Urban Growth Coalition, Urban Regime and most notably Actor-Network Theory[50] – see power in the city this way: primarily based on relationships, not on any particular position in the hierarchy. In the article 'Power and policy networks in urban governance: local government and property led regeneration in Dublin', Paulina McGuirk[51] carefully describes the mechanism leading Irish planners to lose their influence over the city. They simply pulled themselves out of the power network, or rather – because of their passivity the network itself ejected them.

The ironic thing is that, for example in Poland, it is planners and architects themselves who put a noose around their necks willingly and with great commitment. They still try to create an image of themselves as an independent and meaningful force based on the mythical and objective common good. In this image, they are the just defending the common good, which nobody but them seems to notice.

A good example of this was the struggle to save the post war modernist railway station in Katowice, Poland from demolition. To the 'common people' the station literally stank but the only answer the local elites were capable of giving was: 'but it's a historic monument...'.

Planners and architects have no authority or power because they want to base these on something that doesn't exist. There is no such thing as the common good. Every time something like it appears, it is newly constructed by actors operating in networks of power and dependencies. It is time we came back to the discussion about *democracy*. I do believe in the *power of the people*. I do believe that the essence of the city is that it self-manages and that the community not only inhabiting it but also using it should govern itself. But this community is much more than just a set labelled 'people'. It is much more complex because of games and interdependencies between power and knowledge taking place within this widely understood community. Architects and planners do notice their own weaknesses and by demanding recognition of their unique role of defenders and worshippers of the common good, they attempt to justify upping their price. This is morally dubious in itself, but it looks even worse if we see to whom they want to be sold.

For architects and planners, sticking to the distinctive and individually strong players such as administrative apparatus and developers is convenient and profitable but it has little to do with the ethics of social service and public trust which, supposedly, these professions should uphold. It has nothing to do with 'power of the people', and is only connected to democracy because it serves local politicians whose posts were obtained in the process called institutional democracy. It is striking that in Poland, there are almost no examples of planners and architects representing interests of local communities against developers and city officials. And yet Poland has a strong tradition of solidarity and community construction, coming from the 1980s. These are not just anecdotes about architects who designed churches from a table in the middle of the village and with the active participation of its residents. If it was possible for architects then it should be natural and obvious for planners too. But this tradition of solidarity evaporated long ago under the influence of hot 1990s money. Today there is nothing left of either.

To consider power it is to consider the power of agency (but not subjugation). Agency has been the dream of architects and planners at least since the foundation of CIAM (International Congress of Modern Architecture) in 1928. Let us design a square for people to gather, let us design a bench for lovers to cuddle and for pensioners to rest. On one hand, this approach appears naive but on the other hand if we reject it, all we are left with is the utopia of self-organization. If we don't build a house people will build it themselves, if we don't provide a path, people will trample it themselves. Somewhere between these two points of view is the Elemental project by Alejadro Aravena[52], one of the most interesting recent voices in socially sensitive architecture. The idea was in fact very simple – instead of building a house, let's build only a half but in good standard and leave the missing half for inhabitants to build themselves when they need it and have enough time and money.

While we are excited about Aravena's project we should not forget that it was designed for people living in slums and who already had the knowledge, skills and time (and could gradually accumulate materials and money) which enabled them to work on their own houses. I think it is very important to be aware that any material or spatial intervention occurs in a certain socio-cultural and economical context. An attempt to design such a building for big city hipsters or unemployed financial experts from the City would probably have ended in failure.

If we were to search for weaknesses of the modernity project (not as an idea but as practice) then perhaps the movement's fixation on spatiality and materiality is the most significant. It is a remnant of the nineteenth century and its mechanistic vision of science and the world. Obviously, we don't have to automatically reject rationalism, as postmodernism did unwittingly, to find an exit from this mechanistic trap. What we deal with then is space which is shaping us. However, it is much more than just physical space. Rather, it is a material-social plexus which cannot be considered whilst ignoring any of its parts. An interesting example of how buildings change under the influence of political change is one of the tallest buildings in the southern hemisphere: Ponte City in Johannesburg[53]. It was built in 1975 as a luxury apartment building but after the fall of Apartheid the neighbourhood declined and fell under the influence of gangs. The same building, the same physical 'shell' had become something else when subjected to political change. Previously, it was a luxurious destination for South African elites, who enjoyed apartments facing outwards whilst the windows in flats for black servants faced a permanently dark atrium. After the fall of Apartheid it was taken over by local gangsters and later became an abandoned ruin, covered in rubbish up to the fifth floor. Today winds are changing and Ponte City changes with it again, giving a chance to bring it back to life. However, the ongoing economic crisis can thwart these plans. We don't have to search the other side of the world to see how socio-political change influences buildings. There are numerous examples of apartment blocks in Central Eastern Europe which were abandoned en masse by the newly emerging middle class, post 1989.

However, space is not constructed only in this material and legal plexus. Today we cannot ignore the new component: the software that manages an ever-increasing amount of devices is having a direct impact on how (if at all) buildings function. A contemporary bank, an airport and a supermarket cannot function without software and it is the software that makes these buildings what they are.

An airport without software is just a vast waiting room; a supermarket, a warehouse; a bank – at best – a financial advisory centre. These are interesting questions: how is software influencing our bodies? Does it normalise how they function? Is it a disciplinary power or – as Rob Kitchin argues[54] – does it create new connection networks, introducing us directly into the post-human (but not inhuman) reality?

Software is a bit like a magic spell; say appropriate, precisely defined words – and presto! something happens. It is significantly different to natural language, the strength of which lies in inaccuracy, blurring and errors in interpretation. Machine language generally excludes errors. It is a very important difference – all other tangible and intangible elements constituting space are based on natural language. They are subject to interpretation, errors are written into their structure and in fact they allow the liberty of a different point of view, freedom to create your own conceptual structure and write your own narrative.

At first glance, we might try to position software close to other immaterial (intangible) disciplinary tools such as social convention or fashion, but in reality it is something completely different and new in our lives. Its mechanistic and totalistic nature works well with another totalistic narrative – the narrative of capitalism and neoliberalism, which do not allow an alternative. This is modern financial capitalism, as opposed to the 'classic' capitalism in which value of the currency was often based on the gold standard and money associated with the calculated risk. Here two words are significant; both the 'risk' once powerfully introduced into sociological discourse by Ulrich Beck, and 'calculation' which was pointed out by thinkers from Simmel to Marazzi[55]. In the context of constructing space, both minimisation of risks (the obsession with Health and Safety in the UK practically blocks many innovative designs of public spaces) and calculation, being the core of software used inside and outside buildings, have the same result – the reduction of the horizon and cancellation of the outside. There can be no revolution or even radical change without the outside, without what is 'other' and described by a different logic.

There cannot be the outside where there is no border – a crossing line between here and there. This line, surface, membrane and the interface are the key concepts for all narratives of resistance to totality and lack of alternatives, narratives of change and revolution.

Let us return briefly to what is more tangible. Traditionally, the city is shown as a corrupt and dangerous place of evil, a view that originates from the times of industrial revolution. Even if we omit the moralizing zeal of this view, the belief that the rural life is always healthier than the city life persists. It is not always the case and I would even be inclined to risk stating that it is more often the other way round.

The physical space itself can also affect human behaviour. Dieter Frick defines two concepts: spatial synergy[56], as the relationship of thing–to–thing (i.e. building, tree, infrastructure, etc.) and supportiveness, as the thing-to-human relationship, drawing our attention to the influence of things on human behaviour and reactions. Instantly, at first glance the relationship most important in the city – person-to-person – strikes us as missing. However, it is understandable because as the most powerful it can interfere with the other two. Frick focuses on public spaces, seeing them primarily as void between objects which takes on meaning and importance because of objects and people.

When working on my PhD thesis I used a banal but useful tool to describe public spaces: I divided them into those that are constituted by themselves and those that need adjacent functions to constitute them. Obviously, all public spaces can be both but the discussion concerns to what extent they are self-sufficient and to what extent they rely on what happens next to them.

Aristotle wrote that the city educates its citizens in virtue. The city is thus not only a stage on which the spectacle of life unfolds but an active participant in social processes. The city – but what is it? I believe it is urban space understood as I wrote above – as the weave of the material with the intangible, of the social with the inanimate. The city, therefore, is something active, a machine that turns people into 'new people'.

Architects and urban planners of the former communist bloc believed in this power of the city. They reinforced this belief with the socialist intention of creating the new man, and tried to change people's behaviour and break their habits in an attempt to make them better. Planning textbooks explained that the basic purpose of the socialist city's existence was to allow for the full development of human personality. When socialism fell, those old habits, obviously not entirely eradicated, broke out with redoubled force. All things social, all things belonging to the community fell under suspicion and were often rejected. Instead, a little house with a garden became the desired ideal.

Is it possible for the city to change its inhabitants? Or is there some immutable human nature which cannot be changed, and all attempts to do so will end in disaster? Or maybe there are certain habits, culture codes which require more time and better pedagogy to be changed? There are limitations of the body and mind, but wasn't it the aim of the last couple of thousands years of human civilisation to overcome them? Isn't it the story of humanity itself? And has nothing changed in people over the last 2-3 thousand years?

Maybe our loss of faith in the Polis – as the Great Teacher of Virtue – is premature. The city is also buildings. Aaron Betsky says that buildings are the tombs of architecture...[57] Perhaps it is true, but even a tomb is full of potential meanings and activities – to mention only the pyramids or the Lenin mausoleum.

A building is many things: it is a kind of transmitter of meaning and emotion, a traffic generator as people come and go, it is also a symbol that can attract love or hate, sometimes it is simply a big artefact allowing us to find our way in the city. It contains functions which attract some of us and repel others. Buildings influence us – our moods and behaviour – but most importantly they dictate how we move around the city. Buildings (and places) determine where and from people are moving, they attract and repel, and finally they have the power to block people's movements in the city space.

If we treat people as a medium conveying information, then trajectories along which the city inhabitants move become one of the main factors influencing the network of power and knowledge in the city. A man is basically a communicating being. Obviously, the man doesn't usually transfer information in the same form he receives it because the man 'taints' it by making it subjective (this is where the difference between the natural and mechanistic languages that I mentioned before is evident) – but this is still the process of communication. When I mentioned the concept of the pluged-in citizen as the potential methodological tool I meant the plugging in of different people (generating and transferring certain kinds of information) in varying degrees in different parts of the city. In the city then, we deal with the flow of information streams transmitted by various objects – buildings, adverts, people, etc. We can – in different ways and to varying extents – influence all of them. Simply put, we can programme information that flows through the city.

The process of shaping the space on all levels concerns information and its agency, both at the level of strategy – when imposing planning and legal solutions, and at the level of tactics[58] – when dealing with the imposed structure and using it.

Focusing only on the flow of information would clearly be a reduction of the biological aspect of the city – the distance between a bus stop and a shop is mainly the obstacle for our bodies and not to more or less abstract 'information'. Therefore it is worth discussing information and agency – treating agency both in relation to information (as its effect) and separately. Obviously, we know these two dimensions are connected but it seems that it will be more useful to sustain the tension between a separately considered spirit and body than mechanically joining them into one. This tension assumes a gap, emptiness, void that needs to be filled or overcome. As I mentioned before, when considering neoliberalism and software, where there are no gaps and no possibility of multiple interpretations, then totality is a threat.

Thus when strategically shaping the space, its ambiguity

(which in architecture can be definitely treated as the legacy of postmodernism), is also key in making tactical use of space easier for city residents. The ambiguity of interpretation is a fundamental aspect of the human city – as opposed to the mechanistic city. The 'human city' is the city in which people are the medium connecting 'hard', non-human structures. However, these invariant (at least for a while) structures and artefacts – buildings, roads, sewerage but also the legal system and regulations – are both subject to interpretation and its effect. Whatever is built in the city, whatever regulation introduced, it is an activity and legacy of a certain community.

An individual can tactically arrange his relationship only with what a community builds. This is why changes in space (in the widest meaning) must be connected with occurrence of new communities. These communities must be able to function long enough and efficiently enough (agency!) to be able to make changes to city structures. The shaping of space is then directly connected with institution building and/or organisations with a collaborative team approach. The city is a complexity machine, weaving individuals into communal narratives. How to protect individual intimacy in this communal narrative is one of the key challenges for each movement that demands change in the city.

Person

The corporeality of the city is obvious and yet, while immersed in esoteric theories, it is very easy to forget about it. To acknowledge the emphasis on the corporeality of city inhabitants and users should not, however, lead us to ignore the role of consciousness and social conditions. On one hand, it is tempting – following in Latour's steps – to bind the corporeal with the spiritual, to mention the body, the person and the city space in the same breath. On the other hand, however, I insist on unbinding and restoring the singularity, and to focus on the gap which separates singularities. Furthermore, not only singularities are separated but also their properties. This is where the paradox lies, because these properties are defined only relationally; temperature, humidity, colour – they can all be defined because a reference point (or points) exists. Even though a set of certain characteristics describes a certain singularity, it is at the same time a description and therefore something external to the singularity, one of many narratives that restore universalism. To discuss body and the city one has to take into consideration the singularity of each body, each person and every city, and yet, any such discussion is a universalising narrative.

A notion of occasionalism is present in the debate between Graham Harman and Bruno Latour[59]. According to Latour, if a mediator must be present between every single being, then the mediator has the same ontological status as the beings between which it mediates. What then mediates between a being and the mediator? Another mediator? Neither Latour nor Harman give a satisfactory answer to this question. Flat ontology, of which they are both in favour, assumes that every being is equally real. They are different in their strength but not in their quality. I can't agree with this. As a fictional character, Harry Potter is a being defined only by its properties and surface – it has only exterior. However, you, my readers, are much more than that – your properties do not constitute you.

The problem of separation of what is singular can be overcome in several ways. For example, we can assume that every single being is a part of a whole which is projected onto (our) reality. There would be then a meta level on which there would be a 'whole'. This assumption, however, leads us dangerously astray – it would mean that there is something eternal and unchanging, reinterpreted again and again by our world. Is it possible to manoeuvre safely away from idealism but stay close to the individual beings which form relationships with each other? The above mentioned 'reinterpretation' is a word too interesting to be abandoned easily. The word that seems unnecessary in our discussion is 'singularity'.

Beings would then exist both as wholes and as a collection of narratives describing their properties. Each narrative which appears whenever there is more than one being assumes the interpretation as a surplus which properties of the interpreted beings lack. Therefore, there would be a kind of inversion of Badiou's reasoning and consequently – a production of new beings. Therefore, it is not then something finite and constant but a continuous process of emergence of new beings. The gap I speak of is then necessary for this process to occur. Once we know what we need the void / gap for, then we can safely take a look at the popular narrative, connecting everything with everything and how the individual elements are woven together.

The first and most obvious observation is the cultural coherence of the description of what is connected with the body and the city. What is surprising is the almost perfect parallelism of these metaphors. On one hand, there is a physiological reality of the body which is controversial and embarrassing (bodily secretions, secretions of the city); on the other, there is the ecstatic physicality of the rhythm of the city and the rhythm of sex. But in both cases, cultural prejudices and taboos set sex and the city as something unclean. It is probably no coincidence that the Renaissance attempted to both rehabilitate the body and invent the perfect city. Even more interesting is the absence of the body in the contemporary Western city. The Western obsession with purity, sterility and hygiene expunges everything related to excretions (human and urban) beyond the mainstream narrative. And yet we cannot deny our own flesh and the physiological experience of the city. Yet again, here we can see the difference between a building and the city. Today the physiological experience of the city is reduced to the minimum, not only in clean and air-conditioned shopping centres where lifts and escalators allow effortless flow of thousands of people, but also in gated communities and fortress-like office complexes.

One example of a building where, unusually, the architect promised to subject visitors to the corporeal-cultural experience is Daniel Libeskind's Jewish Museum in Berlin. However, it is a building which doesn't really challenge us, apart from the steep stairs, the heavy doors to the Tower of Holocaust, or the play with our sense of balance in the Garden of Diaspora. This building is in fact sterile. Even inscriptions on the walls inform us what we are looking at and what we are experiencing, effectively preventing any unauthorised and unexpected thoughts from occurring.

In the city, whether we like it or not, dirt and effort are almost unavoidable (unless we are moving in an air-conditioned Mercedes, from an apartment to the glass office tower, and back. Although – in this example – can we really claim to even be in the city?). Despite this fact, and also that cities themselves try to limit our corporeality (this compelling story was told by Richard Sennet in the book 'Flesh and Stone'[60]), the classic observation by Georg Simmel that our senses become (over)stimulated in the city remains relevant[61]. In the city, the overwhelming number of stimuli can result in stupor or a kind of trance. It is not surprising then how the city and sex are so often part of the same narrative in popular culture. The city and sex are intense experiences, their physiology intensifies sensations and makes them extraordinary. The contact with other people pushes us back into our bodies, directing us inwards, not outwards. This is where the famous *blasé attitude* as described by Simmel comes in – the excess outside our bodies directs us back inside our souls and the contact with the exterior becomes superficial. This exterior is in fact nothing else but the fetishised public space.

At the centre of discussions about public space is the discriminatory discourse. First of all, there is the question of who under what conditions can access the public space. The gender and sexual orientation perspectives are very important because they mix physical public space with the symbolic public sphere – for example by emphasizing the dominance of a particular iconography and regulations limiting the access for certain groups. Finally, the important part of this debate is the general cultural climate. Can two people of the same sex walk freely holding hands? Could they kiss in public? By asking these questions we are back to these aspects of space which – while not physical – affect its use by the body. From this perspective, we can forget for a moment that the physical dimension of space can also influence how it is used.

The first issue to be considered when discussing the materiality of the public space is – again – its accessibility. One of my favourite examples is Doma Laukums, a square at the heart of the Old Town in Riga. Despite being the central square, it is difficult to consider it as a significant public space. First of all, there is no public transport penetrating the Old Town. There are a couple of bus lines servicing the outskirts of the Old Town but to reach it a short walk is required.

It would be interesting to examine how much time, on average, it takes to get to the Old Town from various parts of the city using public transport. This would become the first and fundamental layer of accessibility. But the accessibility itself – or rather inaccessibility (by public transport) is only part of the problem. The distance from bus stops to Doma Laukums effectively deters those who have mobility problems, such as people with disabilities, the elderly and families with young children. The excluding dimension of the main Riga square is even more increased when we consider who and under what conditions can use it. First of all, the square can be accessed by cars, which pushes pedestrians (all of them but especially pedestrians with young children, the disabled and the elderly) to the position of second-class users. If there are no specific regulations favouring pedestrians over cars, the car always wins. When we finally reach the square, escaping cars on the way, are we safe yet? Not necessarily: there is a pavement surface to consider. Doma Laukums and most of the Old Town is paved with cobble stones which are difficult to walk on, especially when icy or wet. There are only two trees and two benches at the square to offer some rest and shade free of charge. All the other available outdoor seats are in cafes and restaurants.

So whose bodies are privileged on Doma Laukums? First of all, these are bodies of young men and drivers. It is important to add that the entrance to the Old Town is tolled and therefore an economic element of the segregation appears. In a more or less subtle way, very young and and very old bodies, as well as those who want to move around other than by car, are ousted. However, fully-ambulant tourists in comfortable shoes are welcome.

If we see these bodies in the context of the controversy surrounding Riga Pride and the infamous, erotically explicit advertisement greeting travellers in the arrivals hall of the Riga airport (now removed), then the patriarchal and conservative image of the city for the rich appears. What is tangible becomes entangled with what is cultural, political and legal. Before we start to disentangle it, let's take a closer look at another space, another example.

My home town, Gliwice, in South West Poland, was part of Germany before World War II. One of its districts, Wilcze Gardło, still manages to generate controversy today as a surviving and well-preserved example of Nazi urban planning and architecture. It was designed for Nazi party members and officers of the SA and SS, and its most characteristic element is the sports stadium located at the very centre.

It is nothing new, but sport as a social manipulation tool interests me. The positivistic cult of the body-machine is evident here and this appeal of positivism and science is frightening even in contemporary society. Even today many architects and planners still believe that they know best how ordinary people should live. But as in the case of discussion about eugenics (which is arguably not so distant from the contemporary hygiene obsession) it is very easy to be tempted to absolutely condemn this approach. Perhaps this exact difficulty of complete condemnation makes us uneasy when discussing totalitarian systems.

In Nazi urban planning, a man was a part of a larger whole. The fantasy of the organic social structure providing a suitable place for everybody in the hierarchy (because there had to be hierarchy) led to concern for the individual cells, should they begin to degenerate and thus put the whole organism in jeopardy. The state was obliged to care for the health and well-being of its citizens. This obvious idea had its bright side for the favoured 'cells' – healthcare, hygiene and quality of life (it was the Nazis who used standards for living spaces which we still reference today!) as well as the dark side. Cells – people – who were considered dangerous for the health of the nation-organism were mercilessly killed.

In the case of Nazism, the 'quality' of a human being was estimated both from the point of view of the body and 'soul'. In the case of communism, the body aspect was exposed but rather in an admirable rather than repressive way: sport, mass gymnastics, tourism, outdoor activities – these activities were strongly supported by the state.

Today fitness in the Western world is mainly a solitary activity. Individual torture their bodies at the gym, not like in China, where still hundreds of children spill out to schoolyards to exercise together accompanied by music and the elderly meet in parks to practice tai-chi. In the West, mass sport activities are more for spectacle than for physical activity.

In totalitarian regimes both the physical activity and spectacle were present. It is beautifully described by Petr Roubal[62], and he didn't shy away from including in this account a tear, as shed by Czechoslovakian leader Gustav Husak. However, Roubal distances himself from the political aspects of mass fitness activities in the socialist countries. He saw it more as a consequence of Enlightenment rationalism and treating the body as a machine. But however we try looking at this, mass physical activity, organised by the state, will be always associated with the militarization of the society. However, today's worship of the healthy, beautiful and fit body is not so far away from these rational and totalitarian models. This body can be more efficient at work, its healthcare is less costly (even down to cheaper health insurance for those with proof of regular exercise) and in addition, because of the individualised patterns of physical activity, it is also a source of income for a wide range of businesses providing equipment and services helping us to stay fit.

It is even worse – this individualised care that is required by people perfectly fits the perverse neoliberal paradigm of the state, withdrawing from positions it used to hold and introducing much more subtle ways of managing people. Individualised techniques of maintaining fitness have shifted the responsibility from the organism-state to individuals-cells. Each of us, for our own good and for the sake of insurance companies, or under the pressure of fashion, have to take care of ourselves. Instead of being trained by the state we are our own coaches, but the foundations of the training itself and its goals haven't changed. Both the totalitarian state control over the body and control in the radically individualised society are similar, sharing the same rational goal which is difficult to argue with – after all, it's a good thing to be healthy, beautiful and athletic. Besides, we are all free and we can decide if we want to be a part of the system. Or are we?

The triad of the body, the person and space – let's concentrate on the latter.

Most urban scholars, when writing about spatial segregation or discrimination, focus on the place of residence or examine processes of exclusion of specific social groups from certain public spaces. But it is not the perspective of a group, or the place, but the perspective of the individual city user, that seems to me the most interesting. Only from this individual perspective is it worth looking at places and groups.

Obviously, this is not a new problem. In 1980 Donn Parkes and Nigel Thrift discussed it in their book 'Times, Spaces and Places'. Even before that, similar studies took place at the University of Lund. They became widely known when Imię Hagerstand published the text 'What About People in Regional Science?' in 1970. The majority of these studies, however, concentrate on two aspects: either the movement between spaces used by people (home, school, shop, friends, work) or how much time certain activities take. The first aspect is interesting mainly for transport planners, the latter for big shopping centres. I am still amazed though by the fragmentation of these studies. I can still see a much wider perspective which includes the city as a whole, its socio-spatial cohesiveness. I do see a problem with the transition of the analysis of individual behaviour and choices to the analysis of social groups, but it still seems to me that it is impossible to understand the city while ignoring the activities of its people.

In these analyses of spiritual and body entanglements of the city, the question of language remains. I was once told an anecdote about the American university for deaf and hard of hearing students[63]. In its canteen the segregation was striking – black students would share tables only with other black students, and white with white. What is interesting though is that this segregation wasn't a result of racism, but the differences between sign languages used by the two groups.

The language is related to the transfer of information but information is never transferred in its pure form – it also carries cultural baggage. Language in this sense is then synonymous with a kind of cultural community. I insist on understanding the city as the communication machine which also forces communication – communication problems between people stem from different understandings of concepts. We all function in different conceptual frameworks and therefore our understanding of different concepts varies.

Beginning from the cultural/language community, we could next discuss memory, which would help us justify the issues related to the conservation of monuments... and thus we would weave together all these threads into one, impossible to untangle knot. Perhaps it is worth stopping here and returning to the beginning of this chapter. Instead of weaving more threads, we will take a look at the gaps between them.

The question is not: what's wrong with seeing the body weaved together with the legal, cultural and political, but – what of it? How can we weave changes into these structures? (How can changes be introduced into these weaves?). And is it at all possible? Would replacing the cobblestones with concrete introduce more users to Doma Laukums? Would this new surface attract skateboarders? If they appear in this space, how significant will their influence be on the social structure of the square's users? And then, what would be the consequences of this change? Finally, can social segregation resulting from cultural differences be overcome by intervention in physical space?

To some extent, these questions are wrongly put.

When in the city, sometimes we are more a body and sometimes more a person. Sometimes our spatial location is critical, and sometimes irrelevant. And it's not a person as a whole, but the person's properties and fragments that are important in a given situation. It is not the weave that is important, but a specific narrative which positions all beings in a certain hierarchy. The ontological situation of different beings – because of their properties – is not the same; some beings appear, others disappear, depending on how the story is told. This perspective has significant political consequences. Such a narrative, called 'the particular narrative'[64] is used by one of the Polish urban activist groups. We are not interested here in any whole – someone who is a bad guy in one narrative can still be a saint in another. Narratives have to be formulated to achieve certain results. Void between properties guarantees that unnecessary interferences will not occur.

Producing citizens: from socialist to post-socialist urban oppression[65]

This chapter challenges a popular notion which connects a concept of the city with liberating ideologies. Contrary to the slogan *Stadtluft macht frei* [city air makes one free] I present the city as a site of oppression and segregation, taking both as fundamental, inherent aspects of urbanity. Viewing the city as a biopolitical machine, I attempt to analyse incorporeal factors (law, regulations and symbolism) and material factors (spatial structure, infrastructure, and buildings) which shape human behaviour, sustain interpersonal relationships – and in general shape a certain type of human being as a citizen, or user of the city. I raise a question: what kind of citizen or user could be produced by a city using such technologies and who is able to use them in the city? This question is put into the context of the evolution of socialist cities in Eastern Europe into post-socialist, capitalist cities.

Since ancient times, the city has prevailed over the village. The city offered more than just the bare life (zoe in ancient Greek) that rural residents experienced: it also offered political rights. 'For Aristotle's zoon politicon there are no persons beyond the walls of the city; outside the city exist only beast and gods'[66.] Therefore, the city was clearly separated from the village, and, more, from anything extra-urban and from nature. In the words of Mircea Eliade[67], the city was a space of divine order distinguished from a chaotic and profane space outside its walls. This separation establishes a clear distinction between interior and exterior, the sacred and the profane, and between good and evil. It seems a constituent factor of the city. The slogan *Stadtluft macht frei* is therefore the foundation of the city and, like the foundation of a house in archaic ritual, was associated often with a bloody sacrifice – during the Christian era a cult of martyrs still echoed ancient beliefs. Therefore it could be said that from its origins the city was founded on a particular cosmogony, organized according to unique principles[68]. The city is not a neutral space to be socially constructed but a fixed order (but which can be, and is, challenged and changed over time).

These principles and ideological values, laws and regulations limited the freedom of city inhabitants, or citizens, in comparison to the freedom enjoyed by people living outside the city (nomads, vagabonds, outlaws). However, the city not only limits freedom but obviously, also, offers it, freeing people from their clan, family and feudal obligations, allowing them to enter into a new kind of voluntary contract with others (Based on common interests not common ancestry).

In the context of Eastern European cities, it is worth mentioning the existence of a tradition of using open areas, natural reserves and wilderness zones (especially forests) as spaces of refuge and asylum.[69] During the communist period, public spaces in socialist cities were subject to strict ideological supervision and surveillance, always connected with political activities (supporting or opposing the communist regime). It could be said that public spaces in cities were connected with a soul, or the activity of the mind. In contrast, the wilderness was associated with the activity of the body – a view supported and promoted by the regime. This does not mean that in the communist state wilderness was free from any regulations: of course, there were rules, but they were based on common sense, respect for nature and other people (for example: no smoking in the forest). The city-nature opposition stated here refers to the classical distinction between political life – *bio* – and natural and apolitical life – *zoe*. This is what appears to primarily distinguish the city from the wilderness – the degree and intensity of regulations.

The city is therefore founded on a certain system of values and is not a passive field. On the contrary, it is an active set of systems producing specific values. The distinction between what is allowed and what is not is the essential gesture leading to the creation of the citizen. Citizenship is always a privilege; it includes one in the community and, at the same moment, excludes others from the same community. Hence ethnic neighbourhoods or districts built around a certain social status – the ideas behind the City Beautiful movement, or even the famous plan for the reconstruction of Paris by Baron Haussmann in the 1850-1870s superimposing on the dirty structure of proletarian Paris the clean aristocratic boulevards[70] – were incarnations of the same idea: making a division between good and bad, beautiful and ugly. It was always so. In addition, it seems that today's gated communities, execrated by urban planners and sociologists alike, are in fact inherently urban gestures defining what is governed and what is regarded from outside as chaotic. If the city is a regulated – and therefore civilized – area, it follows that the first and fundamental disciplining gesture is precisely the establishment of a border around it (or around its constituent zones).

The consequence of defining the border is to establish certain regulations for the bordered area. Urban public space has always been in some sense privatized, because power was executed by a certain body: municipality, church, interest group, or other organisation. Thus, the contemporary debate concerning the loss and/or privatization of public space seems to miss the essence of the problem. The city, despite its repeated motto *Stadtluft macht frei*, was, is, and probably always will be, primarily a machine of oppression. Municipal regulations such as law, the assertion of normatives and rules, but also social conventions, make this machine. These regulations not only create a kind of negative oppression which is at the centre of David Harvey's[71] and other Marxist thinkers' interest, but also compose the inherent content of the city. The organization of space, buildings, street furniture and plants, is merely a complement to the oppression machine and the physical dimension of the city as an outcome of regulations.[72]

The primary mode of action of the City – the oppressive machinery – is the segregation of people. Beginning with Aristotle and then classical texts of urban sociology[73] such as those by Louis Wirth and Georg Simmel, there is a universal conviction that life in the city is different from life in the village; and that urban citizens experience an entirely different set of challenges and regulations (which shape them into different people) compared to residents of smaller, more traditional settlements in rural areas. As argued in his essay, 'The Metropolis and Mental Life', Georg Simmel[74] sees the city as above all an extremely intense stimulation of the human nervous system, much stronger than that encountered in villages. The city is founded on numbers and on intellect, not on emotions. It is where the money economy comes into its own, with its structural abstraction. The Metropolis described by Simmel shackles human freedom, its instincts, and its life. The Metropolis, then, is founded on the oppression, on the denial, of zoe, or on transforming zoe into bio. Interestingly, the only aspect of the Greek Polis still present in the modern city is the distribution of violence.

The Greek Polis was a small community, a partial democracy based on strong, hierarchical community which cannot be transferred to the contemporary Metropolis (the participatory budget doesn't seem to be a convincing solution). But if there is an existential difference between living in the city and living outside the city, to define this difference is not so easy. However, it is worth trying to create a basic description of the techniques that the city uses to shape its citizens and users. It could be even more interesting to analyse the differences between the techniques used in Eastern European socialist and post-socialist cities.

I will try to define the two main spheres in which the city can discipline and produce its own citizens and users. One is the physical shape of the city: its spatial structure, buildings, roads and other parts of the built and natural environment, as in parks, gardens etc., and the other sphere is a realm of symbols and rules, the immaterial sphere of culture. The physicality of the city exists and affects its inhabitants and users on different levels, ranging from the scale of the city as a whole to the scale of a bench or a tree. The specific arrangements for a space (for example, the technical infrastructure such as roads, waterworks, gas, electric wires, or Wi-Fi) create value for real estate. The physical sphere of the city is then directly connected with the social, economic and political spheres. The most characteristic aspect of the socialist city was its relative spatial homogeneity; as a result the socialist city was intentionally a classless and egalitarian city. The post-socialist (capitalist) city evolves in the opposite direction. Despite declarations of social contingency, the governments of these cities try to push the poorest part of society outside the core of the city, and if possible, out of the city's administrative boundaries entirely. Very often, to justify such actions, or to evade accusations of social cleansing (which have other connotations in areas such as the Balkans), the mythical image of the free market economy is used.[75] In other contexts, the myth of progress might be used, as that against which resistance is impossible. Capitalist cities use elements of the non-material sphere in a similar way, such as through the introduction of specifically and selectively framed antisocial behaviour regulations, as used primarily but not exclusively in North American cities, though recently introduced in Europe (in the UK but also on the continent, for example in German cities).[76] The segregation of city inhabitants is only to a limited extent a tool to discipline inhabitants, however. Urban social segregation explains who is a proper city dweller, and who is unwanted.[77] It does not mean that, materially, the unwanted disappear.

I think it is also important to discuss the difference between methods of disciplining people in public and quasi-public spaces such as shopping malls, or – maybe now – the lack of any significant difference. Maybe the boundary between private and public spaces in the city of late capitalism blurs. Privacy does not really exist. In a given situation – for example living on the border between Israelis and Palestinians – a private apartment is part of a public political manifestation.[78] In fact, anything could become a political or ideological manifestation; and I suggest that the scope of socially acceptable behaviour is much wider in cities (where social control is lighter) than in any small town or rural village. The process of disciplining by neighbours and other well-known members of the society which is often experienced (or is expected) in rural villages or small towns is replaced in the city by panoptical observation by strangers and incidental, concurrent users of the city's streets and other common spaces.

Therefore the city is an environment where we constantly meet the Other, the experience that makes us face the essential dilemmas of post-war philosophy, particularly that originating from the tradition of Martin Buber and Emmanuel Levinas.

Manipulating accepted and preferred conventions is just one of many symbolic methods of disciplining people, yet not far from the most important. The most obvious methods are urban planning and the cumulative development of building regulations, together with regulations of permitted behaviours (for example eating, drinking, smoking, skating etc.), and regulations of permitted advertising, busking, and other kinds of public behaviour. Arguably more interesting than laws or regulations – and definitely less visible and obvious – are mechanisms regulating human behaviour through specific configurations of space(s). Probably the first comprehensive theory (and recommendation for practice) explaining relationships between spatial configurations and human behaviours was Oscar Newman's Defensible Space theory, which he developed in the early 70s. The idea of raising the community through a specific configuration of space and through certain types of architecture is much older, however, as is illustrated, for example, in the eighteenth to nineteenth centuries ideas of British Quakers or North American Shakers.[79]

Newman was a child of the twentieth century; so his proposals are therefore founded on a rational, scientific basis. He introduced a distinction between public space, semi-public space, and private space: a distinction which became a classical configuration of urban spatial distribution. The essence of his idea, which influenced later generations of architects and planners, is a concept that only the ownership of a space, and the consequent supervision provided by a certain and defined community occupying it, could sustain the safe and thriving existence of that space (and hence of the community involved). Newman's concept, in fact, paved the way for today's design practice in neo-liberal cities, based on the conviction that private spaces are superior to public spaces – the idea of public space being closer to that of a no man's land than to that, from another tradition, of the site of common exchange and mixing across class borders (sometimes identified, with little historical accuracy, with the market, or Agora, in classical Athens).

What is even more interesting is that Newman's ideas were based on a fear of crime. And it is this criminalization of various behaviours, and manipulation of the pervasive sense of fear, both from being a victim of crime and from being accused of committing one (as if becoming Kafka's Joseph K), which is one of the most powerful tools to discipline the inhabitants of modern cities. However, apart from fear, there are methods of shaping the built environment to develop positive bonds between people, to support the creation and strengthening of local communities. They are, in fact, rather simple: for instance, focusing on common sense in human interactions, such as allowing people to meet on the occasion of typical daily activities (like going to work, throwing out rubbish, a meeting of parents while their children play, etc.). Spatial marginalisation tends to cause social marginalisation. Space created in a way that helps positive interpersonal interactions increases the likelihood of the emergence of positive social bonds.[80]

In the socialist city, communal, social aspects of space were central to architects' and planners' interests. What was not observed under socialist spatial regimes is the fact that a certain level of diversity could work more successfully in social terms than total unification and homogeneity. There is also an interesting problem of multi-sensual proximity in social spaces. Contemporary architects tend to focus only on visual aspects of city life, whilst, as Richard Sennett argues from a retrospect on cities in Europe and North America since the period of the classical Greek city state (or Polis), in Flesh and Stone[81], city life for centuries was connected with the bodily experiences of hearing, touching and smelling (not simply seeing) other people. This kind of physicality does not really exist in cities today, or at least is suppressed – to be rediscovered by the adventurous cultural geographer or urbanist. People tend to separate their bodies from each other as much as possible, using deodorants, private cars and iPods to do so. In that sense, the socialist city was significantly different from the post-socialist one, partly because of technical delay, and partly because of a different model of development. I would not divide relationships between human beings from relationships between human and non-human actors/artefacts[82] – it is all strongly connected (to follow an Actor-Network Theory perspective – but that is another story). I would argue, still, that the importance of architecture is therefore either exaggerated (mostly by architects, planners, and designers), or underestimated (often by social scientists).

Let us return to the general breakdown I suggested at the beginning of this essay i.e. to the material and non-materiel spheres of disciplining city users. It would be a mistake not to consider them together. Newman's research shows how late-

1960s American housing estates suffered from a lack of clearly defined ownership of space, and eventually degenerated. The same methodology would give completely different results if conducted in Poland or East Germany, or other countries in the old East bloc, in the same period. In communist housing estates the semi-public sphere invaded private spaces, such as private apartments; people spent time visiting each other on a daily basis, watching TV together (because only a few people in one block of flats would have had one). Alison Stenning[83] investigated the alternative social networks that existed during their communist period in Poland in Nowa Huta, and their almost complete disappearance when communism collapsed in the 90s. This illustrates how Simmel's city of money and numbers replaced the socialist city of informal interactions and tacit bonds after 1989.

Therefore, when considering the city as a disciplining machine, it may be helpful to be aware that the built environment and spatial artefacts influence human behaviour only by resonating with certain socio-political systems and the prevailing culture – and not on their own account. Theoretically, one could imagine a city – a mixture of spatial and cultural disciplining apparatuses – as a totalitarian machine of oppression, controlling every aspect of human behaviour. This kind of city would lose the liberating force of the contemporary metropolis, lose its self-organising appeal as a *Polis* and become a kind of concentration camp. But let's be clear – this kind of dystopian city never existed in history, and the socialist city was far from it. One of the reasons is that European socialist cities were never meant to be totalitarian; on the contrary, the essential aim of the socialist city was to liberate its inhabitants. The other reason is that the city is too complicated and since it is inherently governed by many different centres of command it is not capable of operating in such a monolithic way. It is significant that utopian settlements are usually small, thus easy to control by one centre of (usually commonly held) power, and are often (though not always) located away from urban centres.[84]

I would, then, assume that cities will never become parts of a totalitarian machine of oppression, yet always were and ever will be machines for disciplining as well as nurturing their inhabitants and users. The difference between the socialist and the post-socialist European city is mostly connected with the diffusion of power, and with a change in the system of governance. The socialist city tended to be a Fordist city, focusing on the reproduction of the labour force. The post-socialist city is clearly a post-Fordist city, based on the exploitation of a fluid labour force and consumer force, in the context of an economy which is both globalised and increasingly inflected towards immaterial production (or has been so). The evolution of the socialist factory into the post-socialist centre of entrepreneurship was described by Elizabeth Dunn[85] as an attempt to force people to fit the model known in the West. We can easily transplant her way of thinking to understand the evolution from socialist to post-socialist cities. Methods of disciplining urban dwellers have changed and one can argue that instead of a strong homogeneous political system with many gaps, as it was in the socialist city, the post-socialist city is covered by an enormous number of micro-structures of power, united by the ideology of constantly increasing financial gain. Every city is founded on violence and exclusion; the question is how the violence is executed and what for.

Soft and porous boundary

'What is the city?' This question still has too many answers. The problem is not that the definitions we have are wrong. On the contrary, they are all right and each one of them is a part of a different narrative. The narrative to which I was a faithful advocate for many years is the narrative of the city as the contemporary polis. Obviously, I am not its author, nor the only supporter. References to *polis* reappear in discourse from time to time; in Poland the concept garnered some attention between the formation of the Solidarity movement in August 1980 and the fall of communism in 1989. It was a time of interest in conservative democratic ideas, a sector to which the idea of polis belongs.

What if an attempt to reactivate the polis – or even mere references to this notion – is simply foolish? What if it only can lead us astray, to the fantasy land of a conservative idyll? The feature that most clearly distinguished the polis was the clear marking of its border, between the urbane interior and the barbarian outside. It is obviously more a contemporary fantasy than a historical reality, but this familiar division between what is political (civilised) and what is apolitical (natural) dates back to Aristotle. It still affects our thinking about the city and politics today. However, cities have been gradually overcoming this division since the industrial revolution. Borders no longer determine the outside: on the contrary, cities sprawl uncontrollably into shapeless 'urban areas'. Instead, it is the inside that is diverse and divided. Barbarians may have been outside the polis, but they are already inside the contemporary city.

Modernism in architecture and urban planning made an attempt to abolish the border. From the projects of Le Corbusier and Mies van der Rohe, to the late modernist fantasies of Superstudio, there were many attempts to overcome the division between inside and outside. The result was oppression and boredom, combined in various proportions. Postmodernism, by rejecting the heroic, the serious and comprehensive, chose fun and fragment. And where there is a fragment, there must also be a boundary between 'here' and 'there'. The boundary between them doesn't have to be very sharp, but the frivolity with which postmodernism treated it was brutal. Reinhold Martin claimed[86] that postmodernism didn't dispute the boundary as such but the dream of overcoming it, and thus the dream of utopia. He didn't negate the existence of the outside; he simply concluded that it was not worth trying to reach it and that there is no necessary connection between what is inside and outside. In effect, the boundary became a smooth surface, a packaging that may not have anything to do with what it contains.

The iconic building-manifesto of the European modernism, the Barcelona Pavilion by Mies van der Rohe, constructed for the Barcelona World Exhibition in 1928, is a building where space flows freely between the inside and outside. Even an example of late modernism, Ronchamp Chapel by Le Corbusier, contains the element of transgression, mediation between external and internal space. This mediation is only residual: a hole in the wall holds a statue of St. Mary which faces the inside of the chapel for an indoor mass but turns to face outside when the service is conducted outside. The relationship between the reality of inside and outside remains important.

The postmodern treatment of buildings is different. Instead of a consideration of space, it is the image that is discussed. (Obviously, there is postmodern space but it is always monadic – reduced to here and now.) It was Robert Venturi who formulated grounds for this perception of buildings in his famous discussion of 'decorated shed' versus 'duck'. The former is a neutral form with attached information, the latter is a form which is a sign itself ('duck' being an existing building in the shape of a giant duck). As we can see, this argument doesn't concern the mediation between internal and external reality, but only the communication of the interior by means of exterior. So if in modernism the wall was a membrane, in postmodernism it became a screen. If we move from the scale of the building to the scale of a district and a city, the principle remains the same: the border becomes the screen, tied by no necessity with what is on either side. The border becomes autonomous – the true simulacrum. In a less material understanding, the border-screen is the space of the fantasy about the city. This is also the space occupied by PR gurus.

In the European tradition of modernisation as Andrzej W. Nowak rightly argues[87], the border serves, *inter alia*, to deny the fact that the interior is not autonomous. On the contrary; it is a parasite feeding on blood and death. Nowak illustrates this mechanism through the example of Congo where first natural rubber and then conflict metals, obtained and used by the 'civilised world', were at the root of one of the largest genocides in the world's history. The Western world is directly responsible for these crimes but has managed to almost completely eradicate them from European/Western memory and thought. These observations can be directly applied to reflections on migrations in contemporary Western cities. The xenophobic narrative feeds on the conviction that aliens/immigrants are parasites who take the city resources away from the locals – jobs, places to live, food (and sometimes this narrative is complimented by the racist and sexist story of local women being stolen from local men). The creation of the narrative of the border and the division between 'us' and 'aliens' serves to obliterate the fact that in reality the city doesn't possess any resources and that almost all of its belongings are the results of plunder or exchange with the outside.

The contemporary city has lost its physical boundary with the exterior. Instead it has countless and ever growing number of internal boundaries. These begin from spatial arrangements (urban and architectural) that form fragments-monads such as shopping centres, office districts and gated communities, all designed to segregate and cut people off from others. Socially and spatially isolated monads effectively prevent people from meeting the Other.

The disintegration of the city into fragments prevents it from operating as a self-governing subject. The distinction of interior-exterior reinforces subjectivity, however the interior is also disintegrating and therefore subjectivity is disappearing and with it, the city itself. Obviously, we have to be aware that the ability to self-governance is not immanently an urban feature. It is much easier to find – or at least imagine – such a mechanism in a small town or in the countryside. There, as in the ancient Polis, people know each other; they are able to collectively undertake the effort of building the common good. On the other hand, as the unsuccessful experiments of hippie communes from the 60s and 70s[88] proved, small communities are not based on democratic management and egalitarianism but typically on strong individuals, more or less openly subjugating and manipulating the group. It is yet another example of the necessity of institutions as mechanisms transcendent to the community that can give it a chance of survival.

Given all this, can referring to the Polis make any sense today? It seems that the answer is yes. However, we need to be careful that the Polis is not the agora, from which the majority of the city's inhabitants were excluded. If, in my opinion, the self-governance is the foundation on which the city is built, but knowing that self-governance in itself doesn't constitute the city, then is there anything even deeper? Something even more fundamental?

Deeper than self-governance lies self-awareness. Subjectivity. However, does it still make any sense, after Freud and Derrida, to discuss subjectivity? In order to self-govern, the city needs to first be self-aware. There is no place for philosophical digressions – this is survival we are talking about. If the city is to survive, it must understand and get to know itself. By city, I mean the community that inhabits it. From this perspective, can political choices made by individuals, isolated from each other by the conviction of the impossibility of crossing the boundary, become the political foundations of the city? Can these political choices made every couple of years within local election procedures be strong enough to hold city's subjectivity? Obviously not.

The loss of the city's subjectivity can be often found in official development strategies. These strategies involve external development impulses: good things don't come from inside of the city; it is passive and its only task is to be prepared for the invigorating external forces. In this narrative, the city becomes the stereotypical figure of a passive princess waiting for her prince. The princess-city is only a temporary cluster of flows, a virtual being brought to life by external forces. If this is true, then in fact the fluctuation of capital, information and ideas matter, but people certainly do not. This perception of the city should be rejected.

So if no flows, no external stimulation, then what? The key to the development of the city lies in the city itself. The basic assumption that needs to be made is that everyone in the city is worthy, that everyone has something to offer. And more importantly, everyone is missing something. Tensions between these who have and those who need seem to be the obvious driving force of the city. Therefore, there is no place in the city for forgotten areas and isolated zones – each fragment of the city is needed, every inhabitant is required, every communication, every internal flow awakens life in the city. Our first gesture should be the opening of the boundary. Push the internal divisions out. This boundary, however, mustn't become impassable again – it cannot define the city as a closed monad. The boundary doesn't become a membrane again, and neither is it a screen anymore. When there is no screen, there is nothing to project the brand of the city on, there is no space for rating agencies to project the surface. The boundary, instead of being a smooth surface becomes a porous structure, is built of myriad connections, mediations and translations between the interior of the city and its exterior. Instead of the easy metaphor of a wall, it is better to use the figure of a barricade which indeed separates two fighting sides, but also because of its permeable structure allows the two adversary sides to meet and communicate /negotiate their positions[89]. However, the metaphor of the wall is much stronger than the one of the barricade. The figure of the barricade doesn't even cover all the features of the boundary that make it so unique: duality, connectivity/separation and its episodic character (the boundary mediates between certain phenomena, not between the whole interior and the whole exterior).

So we arrive at (yet) another paradox – if the (smooth) boundary of the polis constitutes subjectivity, and the multiplication of boundaries inside the city destroys it, then the question arises: would this plump, cross-fibred zone of mediation be able to reconstruct subjectivity without destroying diversity? Or perhaps, should this new boundary be soft and porous only from the outside and smooth on the inside? Before I answer this question, let us stop for a moment at the internal diversity and pluralism of the contemporary city, qualities that we want to preserve.

The internal differentiation of contemporary cities is primarily connected with the notion of the deprived district. What does it really mean and what criteria determine that a given district should be subjected to regeneration? Hans Skifter Andersen[90] raises two fundamental questions: what does "deprived area" mean? And: what are the causes and goals of regeneration? According to him, many districts in Denmark or Finland considered in need of revitalization would be perceived in other countries as being of quite good standard. It turns out that decisions of revitalization are often politically motivated and connected with the local budgets and ambitions of local politicians. Andersen describes two approaches in European planning theory and practice to deprived urban areas. They are seen as either constituted by poverty or by social exclusion. It is easy to observe that both these approaches are methodologically weak, because where does the poverty end and social exclusion begin?

Let's start with definitions. Regeneration is a set of changes, from the physical form of the district space to the way it is perceived. It can also involve a change in the structure of ownership, privatisation, a focus on crime reduction, or be an attempt to attract businesses and finally it can be the activation of the local community and preventing internal exclusion (for example towards immigrants). If we read the above again, it becomes clear that regeneration is simply the adaptation of space and its inhabitants to some fantasy ideal world of (petit bourgeois?) values. Regeneration is then founded on a particular ideology and the 'dysfunctional' district and its people are simply different to the city standard. Andersen's other observations are also interesting. He writes about the general lack of spectacular success stories from European regeneration projects and argues that without constant stimulation, regeneration doesn't happen automatically (as opposed to the degeneration of a district, when it starts to 'rot' from the inside and this process can be only stopped with external intervention). This observation is in contradiction with the self-healing mechanisms of American cities in the 1960s and 70s, as described by Jane Jacobs[91]. Andersen also points to the lack of unambiguous connections between local processes in a district and the global situation: the city can be economically flourishing and still some of its districts can turn into small, local slums.

A good example of such a fragment-district is Szopienice, a district of Katowice, Poland. There are a lot of good emotions that tie me with Szopienice; in the early 1990s I defended my masters degree thesis, based on a regeneration project for the district. My project was quite innovative for its time and even today I think there are some interesting tropes in it. The idea was to use religion as a tool for regeneration. Perhaps this was rather faith than institutionalised religion, because it wasn't a project of some kind of district theocracy, but rather an attempt to use religious emotions to rebuild the structure and integrity, both spatial and social, of the district. Szopienice's specific character is shaped by its isolation from the rest of the city – its spatial boundaries are defined by a busy intercity road, railway line and post-mining ponds. This isolation makes people form Szopienice not exactly connected with the rest of the city. The steelyard operating in the district used to employ whole families and it also strengthened the 'introvert' character of the district. For these reasons Szopienice could be an interesting example of the tension between the whole (the city of Katowice) and the fragment (the isolated district). What is the intellectual and emotional potential of post-secular intuitions in overcoming this drastic dualism?

The answer to this seems fairly simple and obvious. Post-secular thought allows us to consider a simultaneous attachment to locality and fragment and to a universal urban narrative. Local incarnations of universal deities have bigger emancipatory and unifying potential than local McDonald's restaurants (although the principle, after all, remains the same to some extent). Regeneration carried out only on the basis of arbitrarily adopted standards is almost a totalitarian attempt to standardise people according to visions and interests of the dominant group in the city. The response of post-secular thought indicates to the meta-level, from which standards and interests could and should be evaluated.

Contemporary processes of regeneration are attempting to change people and their lifestyles. The construction of a new man, a common accusation of communism, is now being continued by the neoliberal regime as its enemies are expelled to the margins of societies and cities. Obviously, the very concept of the new man is not necessarily an evil thing – after all, it implies development and a slow climb up the ladder of empathy and humanity. Without the faith that architects and planners can help in this development, these professions turn into a cynical service for developers and politicians. In this context, attempts to understand how physical space influences human behaviour are still interesting and relevant.

Studies provided by Jo Williams on cohousing[92] provide good study material. Cohousing is a type of residential development with a larger than standard share of common spaces. Williams suggests that the spatial arrangement could affect the strengthening of interpersonal relationships but obviously her research cannot determine their quality and 'vectors'. We can talk about strengthening social capital but we are not able to determine whether it would build or corrupt the community. Williams shows that people who are spatially located on the outskirts of these developments are also more likely to be marginalised by the community. When people meet each other in common spaces (such as corridors, car parks and recycling stations) they interact and begin to get to know each other. The smaller the chances of these accidental encounters, the less interactions people have and in effect – less relationships are built between neighbours. The quality of these relationships obviously differs and depends on more than spatial factors, most notably on shared cultural and social capital. It is easier to make acquaintances with people who share a cultural and social background, although a too homogeneous community seems to bore people and actually weakens interpersonal relationships. Otherness – as long as it is not regarded as extreme or threatening – intrigues and fascinates. In addition, the factor of 'rational self-interest' appears: otherness regarding professions, interests and experiences is treated as a chance to build a community of complementary people where a lack of something is valuable.

Population density is a similar case. The more dense, the better – but only to a certain point. There is a demarcation point, impossible to pin down, beyond which people want to get away from each other instead of getting closer. However, density itself is not that important; it is more the gradation of space that is crucial. If there is a distinct buffer between public and private space and public spaces are not uniform (so that different groups can use them simultaneously), then human interactions are of better quality and can occur more easily. Here we can return to our discussion about the boundary as a porous cross sheaf, not a smooth screen. This characterization of the boundary should be considered in the context of another observation from Williams, confirming the common intuition that rich people are less willing to have social interactions than poorer people. This, in turn, brings us to the concept of the a-androgyne[93] – a man seen as a being in which the lack is more important than the surplus. What we are discussing here is then a constant transfer and mediation between beings. The boundary becomes a machine that helps to find connections and interactions which would be the most effective from the point of view of all participants. The boundary is then the institution-interface built by and for city inhabitants but which is at the same time external to them. This isn't anything revolutionary. After all, this book that you are reading right now is external to me, despite me being its author. Therefore, I would like this book to become a boundary/interface/institution /between me and you, my reader.

The tension between part and whole, between a district and the city, exists only as long as there are social groups interested in it. It will not necessarily be the tension between part and whole but only (or maybe even) between one part and another, between one partial narrative and another. A route through a park is not objectively a part of some whole narrative – it is rather the realization of particular interests. Fragment-district is not then a part of a whole by definition and the narrative cannot exist without/beyond it. Therefore, it isn't a conflict of the local versus the city – there is only a weaker narrative versus a stronger one.

Obviously, this doesn't mean that there is no conflict and that everything can be resolved to everyone's satisfaction. On the contrary – conflict is the immanent feature of the city and tensions between different interests and narratives are unavoidable. The question is how these tensions are negotiated. This is the task of the boundary/institution, which on one hand creates the subjectivity of the city, pushing its internal diversity out to the exterior, whilst on the other it becomes a machine negotiating between various internal and external interests. In a way, we could describe the boundary as the utopian machine, because its task is to test different narratives in which certain fragments of the city change their meaning and position.

Urban Multiplicity

If there is no conflict between whole and fragment, but only between one narrative and another, then don't we fall into the trap of postmodern relativism? Is there only a homogeneous multiplicity or is there a hierarchy of better and worse narratives? And if there is a hierarchy, then how is it established? These questions go beyond the issues discussed in this book. The problem is that we cannot escape them, even at the cost of giving answers that may be not fully satisfactory from a philosophical point of view.

At first glance it seems that the best solution would be the pragmatic approach. 'Better' and 'truer' would be the narrative which responds more effectively to problems of a certain time and place. But what does 'more effectively' mean? We adopted the view that there is no one universal interest of whole, but we also declared our faith in the whole as such. Rather, the whole is plural; these are the wholes of the city, of which particular narratives are representations. These representations, however, are not able to describe the one, total, and full reality which is the city. This is also because the city is changing at every moment, and as we established earlier, in the gaps of being the New appears.

It is then the multiplicity of beings that we are dealing with here. Their number can be constantly growing. If so, then the narratives that represent the whole of the city cannot keep pace and represent the Truth of the city. Therefore, they must be told and constructed anew. Efficiency is then evaluated by the fullest (but never final) representation of reality. Efficiency defined as such is inclusive and democratic. We try to include all the elements of the city in the narrative (because it is the only way we can get closer to the truth of the city) and hierarchy is the effect of the constantly changing perspectives. What we deal with here are *wholes* and *hierarchies*, and because they are variable, it makes no sense to insist on an essential advantage of any being or group of beings. But does it really? To what extent are we approaching the Latourian ontological perspective here? Is it 'flat ontology' or maybe something else? Are we really able to take a post-human position without an anthropocentric point of view at its centre?

There are many attempts to define the tasks facing urban planning from the perspective of ecosystems or – as it is often described – from the point of view of Mother Earth. I have to admit that I am dubious about such attempts. Isn't it that the figure of Mother Earth is used by the proponents of this method to picture themselves as her only defenders? Such an attitude wouldn't differ to that of the communist planners who worked with the anointing of 'historical necessity', nor to neoliberal planners seeing their work as the embodiment of global logic (There Is No Alternative). This mindset also resembles elements of the colonial attitude which tries to civilise and sometimes liberate others considered less civilised or oppressed. In order to achieve it, a voice is given to these who are considered in need of representation (or it is the colonists' voice that is imposed on them). This arrogance is unfortunately very common amongst architects and planners – although on the other hand, is it at all possible to go beyond the idea of representation for those who cannot represent themselves?

Before we begin to consider the non-human more deeply, let's see if in our human world we are ready to avoid the trap of paternalistic oppression and arrogant representation. Let us raise this question: to what extent can members of social groups who don't have sufficient knowledge participate in the discussion about planning and managing the city on equal terms with planners and city officials? The governance of the city is a sum of processes, written in specific, sometimes hermetic language, and to understand it education, knowledge and skills are required. How can the city community be a part of processes it doesn't understand?[94]

Fragments of the answer have already appeared in this text. First of all, if there is no interest in the whole, then architects, planners and officials lose the basis on which to claim the position of representatives of this universal interest. If city governance is a heterogeneous sum of processes and if the whole is an ever changing narrative organising fragments in new ways (and thus producing surplus), the language in which the city narrative is told has to change as well. But again – we are not talking about the postmodern multiplicity of equal narratives. In fact, we mean the changing narratives of truth and hierarchy.

If we want to talk about perspectives, then we have to return to the deliberations on gaps between the elements of being. Architects, urbanists, planners and city officials are this gap/boundary/institution, which obviously isn't neutral and has its own agenda and interests (because they are only yet more fragments). The basic function of this gap/boundary/institution, however, is to mediate between other participants in city life (both human and non-human). If we position its existence this way it will not be able to break out of this function. The boundary/institution is constructed by beings as they try to communicate with each other but retain their distinction, while the boundary / institution remains external to each of them. There are several dangers lurking for such a constructed institution. Firstly, how to ensure that it is actually created by yet different actors of the city life? Secondly, how to ensure its relative exteriority to the actors who constitute it? It seems that these questions can be answered at the point of defining the ways of functioning, location and control mechanisms of the boundary/institution.

Specific solutions are likely to differ depending on the context, but certain fundamental features can (and should) be outlined right now, for the needs of this book and the revolution intended by it. First of all, we need to precisely determine the location of a particular boundary/institution (architects – planners – city officials). Obviously, I am aware of the internal differentiation of this boundary/institution and I know perfectly well that it is not homogeneous, not least because of the differences between the various professions (the list of professions being in addition non-exclusive). This internal differentiation is however the immanent feature of the boundary/institution as defined in the previous chapter. It helps to maintain the in-between position while forcing the boundary/institution between the elements of its own diversity. The mechanisms of its own functioning must then on the one hand prevent the boundary/institution from latching onto any actor or a group of actors (this uprooting is similar to the definition of Multitude as postulated by Paolo Virno[95]), and on the other hand it must enforce internal mediations between the components of the sheaf (architects mediating between officials and planners, planners between politicians and architects, etc.). Internal procedures are subordinate to the purpose and function (i.e. the creative mediation) that the boundary/institution is to perform on the surface. It is obvious that the boundary/institution itself is continuously constructed and negotiated. There are no instructions or regulations that constitute it. What defines it is the function that the boundary/institution performs in the city. It is then a being of an open nature, whose elements are simultaneously inside and outside, and they constantly shift and move.

Is a mediator constructed in this way enough to include different city actors in universal narratives? Only in so far that the position of this mediator is a part of the boundary/institution which governs the city as a whole. Let us be clear: the power in the city is in the form of the gap/boundary/institution.

Let us assume that above considerations allow us to construct a basis for inclusive urban governance system – but what about the non-human actors? Are they also parts of the boundary/institution? The boundary/institution doesn't represent any particular social group; on the contrary it itself is just another group, another straw in the sheaf whose role it is to mediate between other groups. The boundary/institution is however something different to a circulating reference (as proposed by Latour)[96]. The boundary/institution is a kind of dialectical being, a mediator, which is both constructed by beings (groups / individuals) between which it mediates, and yet independent to them. If my proposed ontology in which being multiplies by narratives is to be accepted, then the boundary/institution is a perfect example of this process. The multiplication of being cannot then be contained in beings entering relationships – obviously, particular people gain knowledge and skills, social groups grow in numbers, but it still cannot contain the surplus produced in the relationship/mediation/narrative. With a finite number of people, to accommodate the surplus of being, non-human actors have to be included (objects, information, procedures, knowledge). People, objects and ideas coexist and need each other. I am writing this book, using a computer lying on a table, and getting inspiration from the books on the shelves around me and from conversations with my students and other people.

The relationship between the individual/group and the boundary/institution is a hybrid relationship, an example of a phenomenon that could be described as 'social cyborgisation'. The relationship of people with machines – mobile phones, computers, digital cameras or dishwashers – is similar to the relationship between people and the boundary/institution. The critical difference is the significantly greater openness and flexibility of the boundary/institution.

Multiplication of being within the urban community narrative is connected to the process of bureaucratisation. The boundary/institution's structure is spongy – it absorbs the excess but sooner or later this process must lead to the disappearance of the fundamental functions of the boundary/institution. It becomes fully saturated and therefore loses its flexibility and mobility. The only solution to this problem is for the border/institution to acquire the causative function. The institution not only controls and safeguards but primarily produces new beings which are not directly related to it, or to the beings which constitute it. The mediatory function of the boundary/institution is then only a starting point for the production of new social structures. A pathological example of this process is the formation of quasi-nongovernmental organisations stemming from the administration ('quangos')[97]. On the one hand, these agencies are financially supported by the state but on the other, their management and control over them is blurred between public and private. The production of new social beings that I write about must avoid this pathology. It must be based on independency: the source of funding cannot come from the 'mother' boundary / institution, unless the daughter organisation takes over some tasks of the mother institution, together with some of its staff, but then this is a partial reshuffling of beings within new narrative. In addition, the control mechanisms must be transparent for these who enter the relationship and treat the new beings as new mediators.

There is also the third property which the new daughter being (boundary / institution) must have – its function must be different to the functions of its mother–institution. It must really be a new being, not an echo of another being (not another 'echo–being').

In this case, the production of previously non-existent beings is closely connected with the internal heterogeneous structure of the boundary/institution. Architects, planners, city officials, social activists or economists mediate between each other and at the same time they mediate between other city actors. They produce new narratives, narratives that can break existing ones. The ability to continually disintegrate and enter into new relationships is the basic characteristic of the boundary/institution – it is externally defined by the functions it performs.

While we are able to extend the scope of people who should

participate in planning far beyond city citizens – for example we can easily include children in the decision making process[98] – we still have a serious problem with non-human actors. How do we communicate with the grass? In addition, even if we assume that we are able to understand the basic intent of the grass – to grow – we can't really hear it. Our interests are different. It is easy to understand why old, anthropocentric positions, often taken by the religious right wing ('fill the earth and subdue it') – still has the power to seduce.

What kind of relationship between human and non-human actors can be suggested? The Enlightenment and modernist division between civilization and nature is still the norm. This division takes perverse forms when applied to postmodern discourse of ecology. A good example of this is seen in the article by Anne Applebaum about the Nano car[99], produced in India. In this article Applebaum voices her concern that industrial development in developing countries can be a threat to the environment. Obviously, she recognises that Western countries play a part in the increasing danger to the environment but points to 'green' technologies introduced by developed Western countries as the counterbalance to this. What this narrative lacks is a post-colonial perspective. It illustrates the problem with non-human actors; again and again, on either side of the political barricade, their defenders appear and use the protection of nature as a weapon to fight their ideological and political opponents.

Can we then include non-human actors in our human world of politics? Bruno Latour argues that it is possible, although we need to change the understanding of politics and reject the division between nature and civilization. Latour doesn't invalidate the divisions as such (it is, in my opinion, entirely valid to draw right-wing conclusions from Latour's writings[100]); he simply builds networks between actors from different worlds. Our proposal of the boundary/institution may seem a similar solution to Latour's, but it differs in introducing the notion of the multiplication of beings and the rejection of flat ontology. To some extent it also rejects the treatment of science and scientists (or experts) as representatives of non-human actors. Latour does not invalidate the representation but radically democratises it, replacing the representative with a spokesperson. The spokesperson is closely bound with the actor/being and it derives its strength from this bond and from the being itself. The representative is then self-defined, the spokesperson is defined by its bond with beings it represents. Let us take a risky step and recognise the existence of the interior, a sort of 'essence' existing independently of the relationship. The boundary/institution is a mediator, not a representative, but it is constructed by persons and objects. To some extent then, what we deal here with is not mediation, but direct participation of persons and objects (including animals and plants) in city governance. Who creates the narrative holds the power – the gap/boundary/institution has the power but it is constructed by the narratives created by objects, people, information and ideas.

The network of dependencies in which we exist is neither flat nor uniformly dense. It thickens and thins, it has its own hierarchy. Its most fascinating characteristics are not from its egalitarianism, but its volatility. This network is constantly constructed anew. Each actor, human and non-human, is important in the network at a certain time and this is how power is constructed. This power is mainly constructed around the human actors – it is a human that is a subject which is either overshadowed by a tree or walks on a floor made from that tree.

But this power and domination are not given once and for all, and they are not total. For example, let us mention viruses and bacteria ready to kill us, volcanoes and tornadoes waiting to happen, or any other non-human beings and events to which a man loses miserably. We are parts of a larger whole. It is not external to us, this is not some kind of transcendent mother-nature, who requires her own defenders – priests. It is inside this world that we negotiate, all of us – humans and non-humans in our own 'to be or not to be'.

The city community is then constructed as a narrative, which to be true and therefore effective, must be inclusive. The risk of ignoring some beings may be too great – we cannot predict their significance and therefore understand the new narrative of which they would be an important component. The basic constructive elements of urban narratives are boundaries/institutions. Boundaries are located in the void between actors/beings and institutions because they perform specific social functions. However, boundaries/institutions are not defined by what is inside them, nor by their internal regulations and algorithms but by tasks and functions which they have to perform. Exterior acts towards them act as a narrative that causes internal instability, as certain fragments of the boundary/institution are being pushed inside or outside. Each new narrative (if it really is new) leads to the incorporation of new fragments and to the production of surplus – the emergence of new beings. The narrative defines new beings by anticipated effects and by their properties that are parts of the narrative. We don't know what a new being is, we only know what it does – because of the narrative. This is an endless process, the urban community is constantly growing. Hierarchies are changing in consequent narratives as they – or we – try to describe as fully as possible the ever elusive real.

Urban Revolutions – The Manual

Neither social position nor class determines revolutionary potential. It is life itself, our existential situation – security or the lack of it, a sense of fulfilment or frustration – that decides whether we want to make the change. How deep and how radical this change will be depends on how much of our faith in the world as it is here and now, is lost. Frustration is destructive and individual dissatisfaction doesn't lead to social change. To make a revolution is to entrust ourselves to others.

The anti-establishment rebellion is growing among young people who are not able to break into the city and state elites. They often imagine themselves as 'middle class' and they believe they are no different to those who stand above them in the social hierarchy. Their own cultural capital acts against the change, against revolution. The fact that people use the same cultural references doesn't make them socially equal, or equal in their existential situation. The most fundamental and insurmountable difference between those who are secure, and those who are not, those who own, and those whose lives are owned is at the level of existence, at the level of experiencing life – not at the level of values. Our everyday needs and aspirations are buried in the false integrity of culture, religion and value systems. This false integrity, organised around cultural or sometimes religious norms, prevents any real change.

Still, the dominant perspective in urban analysis designates culture as the most important factor that influences city life. This dominant position of culture, the belief in the superiority of 'bio' over 'zoe', has a long tradition dating back to ancient Greece[101]. The consequence of this paradigm results in not only forgetting the social class division, but most importantly, focusing on the immaterial. Instead of the quality of life that is inextricably linked with the body, the intangible and cultural construct of the lifestyle is discussed.

Not everything immaterial is evil. Language and religious imagination should not be ignored when we dream of change, of revolution, of what is beyond the logic of profit. By its very nature, religion constantly searches beyond this world, so the potential of religion is truly revolutionary. Obviously, this may be difficult to believe, especially when observing the Catholic Church in Poland, Spain, Italy and also in Great Britain, but for Christians, Satan is the prince of THIS world. In the majority of Christian denominations, and Catholicism in particular, religion again plays the role of a cultural frame for disintegrating societies. Resigning from its previous role as a creative force which changes the world as it deifies or evangelises it, the Christian church has returned to the position of reinforcing the existing dominant system.

Christian conservatives, whilst critical of neoliberal barbarianism, seem not to understand the mechanism which turns religion from a force of change into a reinforcement of the status quo. It can be clearly observed in matters relating to sexuality. After all, it is the Catholic Church that reduced people to bodies expected to produce more bodies. What else does the Catholic teach on marriage, in which the fundamental value and purpose of marriage is procreation and the rearing of children, besides its obsession for regulating all matters related to sex and intimacy? The Church follows a totalitarian ideology as it tries to control people's lives in great detail – what else is totalitarianism if not that? – and it does so by disciplining the body and sexuality. In this way the Church is complicit with neoliberal egoism, the egoism of the body and desire. Desire and the body is the perfect field of dispute and interaction for religion and the neoliberal regime. When the Church reduces Christianity to physiology, it is, paradoxically, neoliberalism that offers an escape. It provides the dreams of leaving the dirt and escaping into the spirit. Today, these dreams about consumption have become the opium of the masses, allowing them to escape from the fear of unavoidable eternal damnation.

To begin thinking about change/revolution, we need to think first of Good and Truth. Another feature of neoliberalism, the one that it shares with postmodernism, is that it recoils from these concepts. Neoliberalism prefers using notions connected to what is necessary and natural. If *There Is No Alternative*, then it makes no sense to think on what is good or evil, what is real and what an illusion. There is no alternative, therefore there is no choice. Truth is the narrative, which is inclusive for being in the widest possible scope. It is never complete, it is never absolute. The truth that I am writing about is not then the binary Truth of classic logic. To explain, let us consider three sentences. The first one is true: water exists in solid and gaseous states, amongst others. The second sentence is false: water exists only in gaseous and solid states. But what to do with the third one: water exists in gaseous and solid states? This is not a false statement, but if we consider it true, then this truth would be incomplete. It would be the narrative, of which this sentence would be a part of, that would decide on the importance of its incompleteness.

The Truth is then inclusive. The fuller the narrative (representation) describing being (reality), the more true it is. Being, however, is not identical with relationships. Inclusion concerns being, but it doesn't concern the relationship. Deeds are the consequence of the narrative. They cause the multiplication of being. The truth of the narrative is the radical inclusion, the truth of creation. Narrative includes beings (actors), but not deeds. There are better and more true narratives, and they displace worse, deceitful, exclusive ones. Evil exists. It excludes being, therefore it excludes good. Evil excludes, therefore it is a lie.

For being to multiply, there must be a gap, an emptiness, a void. Everything that disentangles and divides allows for the new to entangle and unite. As a result there is more of the new. This in-between – the boundary/institution/void – mediates and changes. Deeds are not being, but they change it. The boundary/institution doesn't represent anything; its 'in-betwe-enness' is relative, is another fragment in fact. The narrative of truth is the meta-structure which gives meaning to the fragments, allows them to influence each other and communicate with each other. The boundary/institution changes the beings between it is located, and in turn, it is changed itself. It doesn't represent the 'authority', 'objective knowledge' nor 'the common good' – it simply allows different fragments to include themselves into the narrative. It alters itself in the process, and the beings which enter the relationships with it. It changes/creates the languages that they use to communicate with each other. The boundary/insti-tution is the radical mechanism of trans-culturalism.

Self-awareness is important. As I wrote before, there is a fundamental difference between you, dear reader, and Harry Potter, who has only properties and is defined by what is outside him. There is no substance of Harry Potter. You, however, are so much more than your properties, relations and the outside. Obviously, your subjectivity is also a kind of narrative, possible only because you are not a homogeneous whole, but because there are gaps in you, there is void inside you around which you built yourself. This void connects you with the outside. This void (in fact, voids, because we are not discussing a void but partial deficiencies) allows you to connect with the world, and therefore, to multiply being. Self-awareness is not unique to humans – animals and organisations also possess it. It is possible that our wait for machines to gain it too is not going to be very long. Self-awareness allows for the active and purposeful (from the 'inside') formation of one's own surface (interface).

The contemporary city, the neoliberal city is frozen in TINA. It almost killed the city but slowly, the ice of the lack of alternatives is starting to crack. However, the source of the deadly cold remains – the one, totalitarian logic of profit. How is this possible, that it so difficult to see the absurdity of reducing life to profit?

Revolution is open to the unknown. Revolution is freedom, it is the pluralism of narrative, breaking with the lack of alternative. Revolution in the neoliberal city would mean to challenge the totality of the profit narrative. It is amusing, because it only requires a slight inclination of your head, a squint, a minimal change in the point of view, to see that friendship, love, the sound of rustling leaves in the park, people rushing on the street and even the gods they carry with them, all of it – cannot be reduced to money. But even as we know this, it doesn't change the way we look at the city. Why not?

We simply have no language to talk about what exists beyond the logic of profit. Money allows different actors of the economy to communicate – regardless of their culture, location, natural language and religion. Money flattens the world, it becomes the one perfectly smooth medium, and similarly to machine language, it doesn't allow for gaps and interpretations. Any other form of communication, any other natural language, is porous. It is imperfect in the transmission of information, but its power lies in the opening of new possibilities. The natural language is creative, whilst money can only reproduce what already exists. The natural language causes the multiplication of being, and thus necessitates the emergence of new methods of communication, because it attempts to describe reality as a whole, rather than reducing it to one dimension.

The foundation of the urban revolution must thus become the 'contamination' of money. The city cannot be reduced merely to a machine producing profit. This one-dimensional neoliberal city has to be challenged and untangled into a series of parallel narratives. This is not about resigning from money altogether, but reforming it by 'contaminating' it. The tax system attempts to impose the logic of social justice on the financial flow, but by doing so, it remains forever external to the money. The real revolution, the real opening for the unknown will happen when other logics/narratives/values become integral components of money, when hybrids combining smooth communication with the creative potential of natural languages emerge. Such hybrid money on the one hand will enable the existence of different logics and value systems, trying to describe reality in the plexus of narratives, and on the other hand, the hybrid money will enable the search for the universal, meta-narrative which gives meaning to the whole. Polyphony is at the obvious core of such a search.

The closer to intimate relations, the more 'contaminated' hybrid money is. It becomes smoother when approaching the surface (interface) of the city, where it communicates with what is beyond the city. The hybrid, 'contaminated' money, contains ambiguous elements – time, emotions, local culture and environment. Hybrid money becomes redeemable only after a series of translations, only after making the effort to overcome the (now imminent) voids within it. The economy of hybrid money impedes the flow of capital (although it doesn't make it impossible), just as the free flow of people is determined by their ability to adapt to the new environment. The economy of the hybrid money is much more closely related to what is alive and real.

Revolution will not happen without the boundary/institution which untangles and negotiates. But most importantly – it weaves and creates. It is a manufacturer of the new. To build the boundary/institution is the act of revolution itself.

It is time to summarise and clearly present the basic assumptions and objectives of the urban revolution.

First of all: the city is a subject, and the world is the resource. Today, the opposite is true; it is the city that is the resource for the global markets. This should be reversed. The city users have to be bound, their lives and interests linked with specific localities. Globalism should not be rejected – it has to be used. The city must – through the porous boundary/institution – negotiate with what is beyond it. The city must produce and control the production of what it needs to survive. Plugged-in citizenship is one of the ways in which the city can be empowered and regain its subjectivity while remaining open to the world.

Secondly: the city belongs to all those who want to come to it and offer it something. Everyone is entitled to any city, on the condition that they devote to it their time, attention, commitment and work. The city belongs to all, but not in the same way. But it is this intimate relationship with the city which is more important than the power of the financial flow. When people move from place to place, they have to learn a new environment, adjust to the new place (and also give the new place time, to adjust to themselves in turn). The same applies to capital. The boundary/institution changes both those who come to it, and those to whom it comes. No one is excluded from this process.

Thirdly: what is material is more important than the abstract. Money is the language used by actors of the market. The market is global, the actors are global, but the city is not. Thus the city must be protected, its materiality and its biological dimension, from the abstract and everything that is unrelated to either its locality or life. Money has to be 'contaminated' with locality and new money-hybrids must be created.

Fourthly: the logic of the city is different to the logic of the global market. The city operates in a different rhythm and has different goals to a business enterprise. The city, its inhabitants and users and their long-term interests, should have the absolute priority over the short-term interests of businesses. The city itself is not one homogeneous narrative; it is a polyphonic and complex narrative in which individual threads constantly negotiate with each other to establish their importance and position.

Finally, life is more important than profit. Profit is only one of many possible city narratives and it describes only a very small fragment of reality. The world and life can be neither reduced to profit, nor equated to it. The naked life, *zoe* – food, health, accommodation – should not be considered a source of profit.

To start the revolution is to see the world differently. Slightly incline your head, squint your eyes and see – it is all already there. Now, start believing in what you just saw.

Notes

1. Alvin Toffler is mainly known as the author of 'The Third Wave' in which he describes a world without mass production and mass dwelling.

2. Glaeser, Edward (2011) Triumph of the City, Macmillian: Oxford; Ellin, Nan (2006) Integral Urbanism, Routledge: New York; Scott, Allen J. (2008) Social Economy of the Metropolis. Cognitive-Cultural Capitalism and Global Resurgence of Cities, Oxford: Oxford

3. City as a political idea (Plymouth 2011).

4. At the beginning of the 90s his books were very popular among American conservatives especially those gathered around the intellectual leader of the Republican Revolution, Newt Gingrich.

5. To mention only Barcelona and Florence.

6. World's richest 100 cities generate around 25% of global GDP: http://www.citymayors.com/statistics/richest-cities-gdp-intro.html [As on 29 July, 2011]

7. http://www.state.gov/r/pa/ei/bgn/5444.htm [As on 23 November 2011]

8. These two cities were described in the book by Heiko Schmid 'Economy of Fascination: Dubai and Las Vegas as Themed Urban Landscapes' Gebruder Borntraeger: Berlin, 2009.

9. Chad Haines writes about the latest history of Dubai and its current situation in the chapter 'Crack in the Facade: Landscapes of Hope and desire in Dubai' of the book 'Worlding Cities: Asian Experiments and the Art of Being Global', Ananya Roy and Aihwa Ong.

10. O'Brien, Richard (1992), Global Financial Integration: The End of Geography, New York: Council on Foreign Relations Press.

11. http://my-poznaniacy.org/ [As on 24 July 2011]
12. Wellman, Barry. Hampton N. Keith. The not so global village of Netville. In Barry Wellman and Caroline Haythornthwaite (Eds.) (2002). The Internet and Everyday Life. Oxford, UK: Blackwell.
13. Short story 'Linia oporu' in collection 'Król Bólu', Wydawnictwo Literackie, Kraków 2011.
14. Senett, Richard (1994) Flesh and Stone. W.W.Norton and Co. London and New York.
15. Krzysztof Nawratek, City as a Political Idea. (Plymouth: Plymouth University Press, 2011).
16. Jane Jacobs in her book 'Economy of Cities' writes about mechanisms connecting the industrial production with development of infrastructure. Jacobs uses the term 'import replacement' to describe the process of internalisation by the city of previously imported goods. Sharon Zukin wrote mainly about the meaning of culture as the element of growth in post-industrial cities. Edward Glaeser is the author of the term 'non-market social interactions', proving that economical development cannot take place without elements which are not a part of the market economy.
17. Compare with Jacek Dukaj, Lód (Kraków 2007), page 451: 'There is no creation in the truth, to tell the truth is to replicate, to copy, to repeat after the world – what is the satisfaction from the mindless newspaper report? Nothing, just talk. But – to lie...! To lie means to add something from yourself, to insert into their view of the world your own mind's creations, to bring non existent people, objects and events to life.'
18. Bloom Harold (1997) The Anxiety of Influence. A theory of Poetry. Oxford University Press: Oxford and New Work.
19. Hirst, Paul (2005) Space and Power. Politics, War and Architecture. Polity Press: Cambridge, page 25.
20. Parks set up by residents – not always legally: http://nasz

park.pl/index.php [As on 23 November 2011].

21. Harvey Cox, Secular City: Secularization and Urbanization in Theological Perspective, pp 150 – 166. (New York: Macmillan, 1966).

22. Zoe in ancient Greek.

23. Christian Norberg-Schulz, Genius Loci, Towards a Phenomenology of Architecture. (New York: Rizzoli, 1980.) Christopher Alexander, A pattern language: Towns, buildings, construction. (Oxford University Press, 1977.) Juhani Pallasmaa, The Eyes of the Skin. Architecture and the Senses. (New York: John Wiley, 2005.) Marc Auge, Non Place. (London: Verso, 1995.)

24. Martin Heidegger, Building, Dwelling Thinking, in Neil Leach (ed.) Rethinking Architecture. A reader in Cultural Theory, pp: 100 – 109. (London: Routledge, 2008).

25. The plan of Rome, made in 1748 by Italian architect and cartographer Giambattista Nolli. The plan defines two types of space – private and public. Public space is defined not only as squares and streets but also interior of churches and other public buildings. The Nolli plan was very popular in the late 70s mainly due to the Roma Interotta competition (1978) in which famous architects (Piero Sartogo, Constantino Dardi, Antoine Grumbach, James Stirling, Paulo Portoghesi, Romaldo Giurgola, Venturi and Rauch, Colin Rowe, Michael Graves, Rob Krier, Aldo Rossi and Leon Krier) were invited to work on projects with the Nolli Plan as the starting point. Today the plan is regarded as the fundamental document that defines the basis of our under-standing of urban space.

26. Oscar Newman, Defensible Space. (New York: Macmillan, 1972).

27. Richard Sennett, The Conscience of the Eye: The Design and Social Life of Cities. (New York: Alfred A. Knopf, 1990).

28. Newman's vision is surprisingly idealistic; it strongly

rejects class tensions and positions itself close to the conservative, Christian (or even Catholic) vision of organic community. As he writes in his book 'Creating Defensible Space', p.41. (Washington, D.C.: U.S. Department of Housing and Urban Development Office of Policy Development and Research, 1996.): 'The division of the community into smaller communities neighboring the aim of enhancing interaction between neighbors. Parents watching children playing will be better acquainted. They will not feel trapped in their homes, forced to cope alone with adversity. Tension between landlords and their tenants, the problems with unruly behavior, will most likely disappear, if they both will live down the street, get to know each other better and be able to learn how to properly act towards each other.'

29. This is my free interpretation of Badiou's void as a gap between situation and representation. If identity is a kind of representation of a particular reality, built primarily on language, then it is obvious that an individual identity is not capable of representing the whole subject. Between these identities the unrepresented being / reality exists. Void in Badiou's philosophy is anything but empty.

30. Christian Norberg-Schulz, Genius Loci: Towards a Phenomenology of Architecture. (New York: Rizzoli, 1980).

31. More about the Nazi interpretation of Heidegger's philosophy in architecture can be found in the essay by Neil Leach 'Dark side of the Domus' (in What is architecture? edited by Andrew Ballantyne, Routledge 2002, pp. 88 - 102).

32. Sensory deprivation experiments have been conducted since 1950s (however, the phenomenon was known much earlier), mainly by Donald O. Hebb at the McGill university in the USA (this research was partly financed by the CIA). The techniques implementing sensory deprivation were probably used during interrogations on the both sides of the

Iron Curtain. John C. Lily invented the isolation tank, a soundproof, lightless tank inside which subjects float in salt water at body temperature. In effect, without external stimuli, the brain starts to simulate them, producing visual, sound and touch hallucinations. More about sensory deprivation: John Rasmussen, Man in Isolation and Confinement. (New Jersey: Aldine Transaction, 2007).

33. I refer here to the conviction related to flat ontology, that there is no difference between different categories of being, that man, a tree and a prime number should be treated in the same way. However, it is not categories of being that are important, but the relationships between them.

34. Manuel De Landa, A Thousand Years of Nonlinear History. (New York: Zone Books, 1997).

35. E. M. Cioran, Encounter with the Void, The Hudson Review, Vol. 23, No. 1 (Spring, 1970), pp. 37-48.

36. E. M. Cioran, Mechanism of Utopia, Grand Street, Vol. 6, No. 3 (Spring, 1987), pp. 83-97.

37. Sicinius: What is the city but the people?; Citizens: True, The people are the city., Coriolanus, Act 3, scene 1.

38. Krzysztof Nawratek, City as a Political Idea. (Plymouth: Plymouth University Press, 2011).

39. Paulo Virno in his book A Grammar of the Multitude (Semiotext(e), 2004), at the very beginning (pp. 21 - 26) explains the difference (referring to Hobbes and arguing with him) between 'the people' as a singleness, always connected with the state, and the 'multitude / plurality' as something that exists outside the country politically and against individuality. For Hobbes, this 'multiplicity' – frighteningly for him – is the state of nature, but for Virno it is the only chance to go beyond the liberal tradition of the nation state.

40. Assemblage is a very popular concept of Manuel De Landa. See: Manuel De Landa, A New Philosophy of Society:

Assemblage Theory and Social Complexity (Continuum, 2006) Assemblage literally means a collection, but its primary meaning today is an organization founded without a preliminary structure (a plan, intention, or the physical structure of the institution as such).

41. Harvey Cox explained the processes of secularization in compliance with the essence of Christianity in reference to the famous passage from St. Paul. See: Harvey Cox, The Secular City, p.10. (New York: Macmillan, 1966.) In a different context Alain Badiou also referred to the essence of Christianity, using the same quote, to reject the postmodern difference, and to call for universal space and the law, without taking into consideration cultural specificities.

42. The Other, as in Martin Buber's philosophy.

43. An introduction to Alain Badiou's philosophy: Christopher Norris, Badiou's Being and Event. (New York: Continuum, 2009).

44. A fictional character from the Moomins children's books series by Tove Jansson. This quotation is from the book Moominland Midwinter.

45. All this fragment is my free interpretation of Alain Badiou's thought.

46. The results of Koolhaas' work can be found in the film Koolhaas / Lagos (2002) and in the book Lagos: How it works (2007). Rem Koolhaas is considered one of the greatest and most influential contemporary architects. His works include not only buildings, but also books and research. In Lagos he observed the city; it experienced its heyday in the 1970s and today is a concrete jungle, in which people try to survive. Koolhaas delights in the struggle for survival – for example, that along the mile-long queues of cars a kind of mobile market has emerged, offering different products to motorists trapped in cars.

47. Mainly Paolo Virno, Franco „Bifo" Berrardi and Christian

Marazzi.

48. His book Rhythmanalysis: Space, Time and Everyday Life (London: Continuum, 2004) is about the rhythm of the city.

49. I use the concept of the common good in a very narrow meaning as used by architects and urban planners. The genesis of such an understanding of this notion are the conclusions of the influential article 'The tragedy of the commons' published in 1968 by Garrett Hardin. The main thesis of the article was that the free exploitation of natural resources by multiple actors' self-interest leads to the destruction of these resources and that this is despite the actors' awareness of the consequences of their actions. Hardin believed that there are two solutions to this dilemma – either privatization or strong government regulations. It should be added that Elinor Ostrom (winner of the Nobel Prize in Economics in 2009) draws attention to the self-regulated community, if it is territorially connected with specific resources. We should also be aware that the concept of common good is much wider and has a long tradition – for example, the Catholic social teaching focuses on the conditions in which the human person can realize fully his perfection, in the tradition of the Italian autonomists (with the aforementioned Paolo Virno, Maurizio Lazzarato and Antonio Negri) the common good links with the notion of the general intellect, the concept of immaterial labor and the debate on the appropriation of the capital of such spheres as language or common knowledge.

50. Theories of urban management – mainly these originated in the United States (especially the first two). All involve the fragmentation of power in the post-industrial city. In a nutshell, Growth Coalition involves the action of a centralised group of major players in the city (mostly landowners) who, through simulations of economic growth, aim to increase the value of their land and property. In this theory,

an extremely important role is played by the local media that serves the local elite as a kind of 'propaganda office for city growth'. The Urban Regime involves the cooperation of more weaker actors who by acting together overcome their weaknesses.

51. McGuirk, P.M. (2000) Power and policy networks in urban governance: Local government and property-led regeneration in Dublin, Urban Studies, Vol. 37 (4), pp. 651-672.

52. http://www.alejandroaravena.com/obras/vivienda-housing/elemental/

53. http://www.wolagiewicz.com/story/1

54. Dodge M, Kitchin R (2009) Software, objects, and home space, Environment and Planning A 41(6) 1344 –1365.

55. Christian Marazzi, Capital and Language: From the New Economy to the War Economy. (Los Angeles: Semiotext(e), 2008).

56. Dieter Frick, Spatial Synergy and Supportiveness of Public Space, Journal of Urban Design, Vol. 12. No. 2, 261–274, June 2007.

57. Aaron Betsky, Architecture beyond buildings, 2008. Online [accessed 27 June 2011] http://www.moleskine.com/moleskinecity/focus_on/architecture_beyond_the_building.php

58. I refer here to the division made by Michel De Certeau in The Practice of Everyday Life. (Berkeley: University of California Press, 1984).

59. Graham Harman is an American philosopher, associated with Speculative Realism. The discussion was held at the London School of Economics in 2008. Bruno Latour, Graham Harman, Peter Erdelyi, The Prince and The Wolf. Latour and Harman at the LSE. (Winchester: Zero Books, 2011).

60. Richard Sennett, Flesh and Stone: The Body And The City In Western Civilization (New York: Norton, 1994).

61. "Georg Simmel, The Metropolis and Mental Life, 1903.

62. After 24 minutes of the performance, parents, carrying their

3- to 6-year-old children, filled the stadium. During the 8 minutes of the performance, the children 'exercised' with their mothers, jumping around them, marching with them, dancing with them and riding on their backs. Accompanied by passionate applause, the children left the stadium on the (right) shoulder of their mothers, waving to the crowd with white scarves. Husák wiped away a tear" Roubal, P. Politics of Gymnastics: Mass Gymnastic Displays Under Communism in Central and Eastern Europe. Body & Society June 2003 9: 1-25.

63. Gallaudet University in Washington, D.C. http://www.gallaudet.edu/

64. Kacper Pobłocki explains in the interview: "The starting point is what Lech Mergler calls 'a particular narrative'. The narrative is based on a specific focus on the real problems of the inhabitants of the city and stands in opposition to the majority of Polish politics, which revolves around the symbolic politics. While the ideological conflicts are to some degree relevant, their importance was a little exaggerated. In addition to such discussions as the abortion issue (for or against the right to choose), the death penalty (for or against), homosexual marriages (for or against), there is a whole spectrum of topics and issues that are not dealt with. Moreover, those who are polarized on ideological issues on the level of the particular narrative have common postulates. A common ground is often greater than what divides them. We have a situation where people are divided into different ideological corners according to symbolic conflicts and the real problems are pushed away. I find that when 'My Poznaniacy' (the urban activist group) don't talk about symbolic issues, a much wider collaboration is possible. People labelled as left or right, not only can but also want to cooperate." Notes na 6 tygodni, 68 / 06-07.2011, Bec Zmiana, pages 155 – 156.

65. This chapter was published in Miles, M. Savage, J. 2012, Nutopia. A Critical view of future cities, Plymouth: Plymouth University Press, pp. 36-46.

66. McLean, G. F., Kromkowski J., 1991, Urbanization and Values (Cultural Heritage and Contemporary Change Series I Culture and Values) p. 169, Washington, The Council for Research in Values in Philosophy.

67. Eliade, M., 1968, The Sacred and the Profane: The Nature of Religion, Philadelphia: Harvest Books.

68. Rykwert, J., 1988, The Idea of Town, Princeton: Princeton University Press.

69. Weiner, D. R., 1999, The Little Corner of Freedom: Russian Nature Protection from Stalin to Gorbachev, Berkeley (CA), University of California Press.

70. Harvey, D., 2006, The Political Economy of Public Space, in Low, S. and Smith, N., The Politics of Public Space, New York: Routledge.

71. Harvey, D., 1973, Social justice and the City, London, Edward Arnold.

72. Mumford, L., 1965, 'Utopia, the City and the Machine', Daedalus, 94, 2, 271-292.

73. Simmel, G., 1950, The Sociology of Georg Simmel, New York: Free Press, pp.409-424.

74. Ibid.

75. Bollens, S., 2001, 'City and Soul. Sarajevo, Johanesburg, Nicosia', City, 5, 2, 169-87.

76. Bernd, B., 2007, 'From Disciplining to Dislocation. Area Bans in Recent Urban Policing in Germany,' European Urban and Regional Studies, 14, 321.

77. Beckett, K. and Herbert, S., 2008, 'Dealing with disorder. Social control in the post-industrial city,' Theoretical Criminology, 12, 1, 5-30.

78. Kallus, R., 2004, 'The Political Role of Everyday', City. 8, 3.

79. Nicoletta, J., 2003, 'The Architecture of Control: Shaker

Dwelling. Houses and the Reform Movement in Early-Nineteenth-Century America', The Journal of the Society of Architectural Historians, 62, 3, 352-387.

80. Williams, J., 2005, 'Designing Neighbourhoods for Social Interaction: The Case of Cohousing,' Journal of Urban Design, 10, 2, 195 – 227.

81. Sennett, R., 1995, Flesh and Stone, London, Faber and Faber.

82. Frick, D., 2007, 'Spatial Synergy and Supportiveness of Public Space', Journal of Urban Design, 12, 2, 261 – 274.

83. Stenning, A., 2007, 'Wypieranie stali: Myśląc o Nowej Hucie poza hutą,' in Kaltwasser, M.,Majewska, E., Szreder, K., Futuryzm Miast Przemysłowych – 100 lat Wolfsburga i Nowej Huty, Kraków (PL), Ha! Art.

84. Miles M., 2008, Urban Utopias: the built and social architectures of alternative settlements, London, Routledge.

85. Dunn, E., 1998, Privatizing Poland, Ithaca (NY), Cornell University Press.

86. Reinhold Martin, 2010, Utopia's Ghost: Architecture and Postmodernism, Again. London: University of Minessota Press.

87. Andrzej W. Nowak, Europejska nowoczesność i jej wyparte konstytuujące 'zewnętrze', Nowa Krytyka, 26/27 2011, pp: 261-291.

88. Most examples of this type of commune collapsed after a few months.

89. http://www.adbusters.org/magazine/94/barricades.html [11 July 2011].

90. Hans S. Anderson, Can Deprived Housing Areas Be Revitalised? Efforts against Segregation and Neighbourhood Decay in Denmark and Europe, Urban Studies April 2002 vol. 39 no. 4, pp: 767-790.

91. The classic work of Jane Jacobs, The Death and Life of Great American Cities from 1961 is an anti-modernist manifesto, showing (mainly through the example of Greenwich Village

in New York) the relationship of social dynamics and vitality with spatial mix of different functions and small scale urban tissue (mainly in the small scale of quarters and dense network of streets).

92. Jo Williams, Designing Neighbourhoods for Social Interaction: The Case of Cohousing, Journal of Urban Design, 10/2005, pp: 195-227.

93. This is the key idea from my book City as a Political idea.

94. There are many books and articles on social participation in urban planning, in which this question is asked. Answers almost always come down to listening to people and educating them. Education, however, involves the imposition of language – that is the way of thinking – by the experts (planners, architects, civil servants) on the non-professional community. It seems obvious that if one accepts that in the process of learning the language takes place in two directions at once, then a change in the language used by professionals should occur (in fact, the language should be constantly changing). This means continuous 'rewriting' of the existing regulations and opening up the institutions (which is in fact one of the main demands of this chapter).

95. 'We have said that the multitude is defined by the feeling of not-feeling-at-home, just as it was defined by the consequent familiarity with "common places," with the abstract intellect.' Paolo Virno, A Grammar of the Multitude, p. 40. (Los Angeles: Semiotext(e), 2004).

96. A circulating reference is the formation of networks between different actors during research. The border/institution is much more stable than a circulating reference. Similarly, it is constructed by what is external to it, but in contrast it becomes an independent being.

97. Quangos (quasi-autonomous non-governmental organisation) – organizations set up by the government (mainly in the UK) 'pretending' to be NGOs. Following the 2008 publi-

cation by the Taxpayers' Alliance report alleging these organizations wasted billions of pounds, the government of David Cameron (after coming to power in 2010) began to abolish these organizations.

98. See for example: Jill Swart Kruger, Louise Chawla, 'We know something someone doesn't know': children speak out on local conditions in Johannesburg. Environment &Urbanization Vol 14 No 2, October 2002

99. http://www.slate.com/id/2182075/ [17 July 2011].

100. Bruno Latour mentions the possibility of such an interpretation of his work in a discussion with Graham Harman. Bruno Latour, Graham Harman, Peter Erdelyi, The Prince and The Wolf. Latour and Harman at the LSE, p.94. (Winchester: Zero Books, 2011).

101. As defined by Foucault based on his analysis of Aristotle: 'Zoe', the naked life and 'bio' – the naked life elevated by the participation in the political life.

Contemporary culture has eliminated both the concept of the public and the figure of the intellectual. Former public spaces – both physical and cultural – are now either derelict or colonized by advertising. A cretinous anti-intellectualism presides, cheerled by expensively educated hacks in the pay of multinational corporations who reassure their bored readers that there is no need to rouse themselves from their interpassive stupor. The informal censorship internalized and propagated by the cultural workers of late capitalism generates a banal conformity that the propaganda chiefs of Stalinism could only ever have dreamt of imposing. Zer0 Books knows that another kind of discourse – intellectual without being academic, popular without being populist – is not only possible: it is already flourishing, in the regions beyond the striplit malls of so-called mass media and the neurotically bureaucratic halls of the academy. Zer0 is committed to the idea of publishing as a making public of the intellectual. It is convinced that in the unthinking, blandly consensual culture in which we live, critical and engaged theoretical reflection is more important than ever before.